PALESTINIAN REFUGEES AND INTERNATIONAL LAW
Assistance, Protection and Durable Solutions

PALESTINIAN REFUGEES AND INTERNATIONAL LAW

The International Legal Framework
Governing Assistance, Protection and
Durable Solutions

Palestinian Refugees and International Law:
A Study on the International Legal Framework Governing Durable Solutions,
Aid, Protection and the Right of Return of Palestinian Refugees

ISBN (13) (Paperback): 978-1-68109-022-1
ISBN (10) (Paperback): 1-68109-022-8
ISBN (13) (Kindle): 978-1-68109-023-8
ISBN (10) (Kindle): 1-68109-023-6
ISBN (13) (ePub): 978-1-68109-024-5
ISBN (10) (ePub): 1-68109-024-4

NOTE: The names and/or other details of refugees photographed in this study have been altered to protect their identities and security.

About the Imprint

The mission of Time Books™ is to reintroduce time-tested values and truths to modern debates on political, economic, and moral issues. The imprint focuses on books and monographs dealing with society, ethics, and public policy.

The *Refugee Rights* Series™ of Time Books™ publishes monographs and treatises discussing the laws and public policies surrounding contemporary refugee issues. Complete your collection with the following titles:

- *Introduction to the Global Refugee Framework: An International Legal Perspective*
- *Palestinian Refugees and International Law*
- *Hope and a Future: The Story of Syrian Refugees*

TIME 🏛 BOOKS

Conspectus

Detailed Contents

Detailed Contents   15

Abbreviations

CDHRI	Cairo Declaration on Human Rights in Islam
CEDAW	Convention on the Elimination of all Forms of Discrimination against Women
CESCR	UN Committee on Economic, Social and Cultural Rights
CPIUN	Convention on the Privileges and Immunities of the United Nations (1946)
CRSR	Convention Relating to the Status of Refugees (1951)
GA	General Assembly (of the UN)
HRC	UN Human Rights Committee (of the ICCPR)
IASC	Inter-Agency Standing Committee
ICCPR	International Covenant on Civil and Political Rights
ICERD	International Convention on the Elimination of All Forms of Racial Discrimination
ICESCR	International Covenant on Economic, Social and Cultural Rights
IDF	Israeli Defense Forces
OHCHR	Office of the UN High Commissioner for Human Rights
OIC	Organisation of Islamic Cooperation
oPt	Occupied Palestinian territories
PA	Palestinian Authority
PLO	Palestine Liberation Organization
Refugee Convention	Convention Relating to the Status of Refugees (1951)
Refugee Protocol	1967 Protocol Relating to the Status of Refugees
SC	Security Council (of the UN)
UDHR	Universal Declaration of Human Rights
UN	United Nations
UNAT	United Nations Appeals Tribunal
UNCCP	UN Conciliation Commission for Palestine
UNCRC	UN Convention on the Rights of the Child
UNDT	United Nations Dispute Tribunal
UNHCR	Office of the United Nations High Commissioner for Refugees
UNHRC	United Nations Human Rights Council
UNRWA	UN Relief and Works Agency for Palestinian Refugees in the Near East
VCDR	Vienna Convention on Diplomatic Relations (1961)

Chapter 1. Historical Overview of the Palestinian Refugee Problem

A. The Roots of the Modern State of Israel

The roots of the modern State of Israel can be traced back to nineteenth and twentieth-century Zionism. Dr. Theodor Herzl, the main architect behind the Zionist movement, argued that the only solution to anti-Semitism, which was pervasive in nineteenth century Europe, was the establishment of a Jewish state. The First Zionist Congress was held in Basel, Switzerland, in 1897, to search ways to legally establish a Jewish state in Palestine. At the time, the indigenous population of Palestine was 92% Arab (Muslim and Christian), with Jews and other groups constituting 8% of the population.

After the Basle Congress, the Zionist movement approached the British government to support the creation of a Jewish state. In the midst of World War One, the British found Jews to be helpful allies and embraced their cause. The support of the British culminated with the 2 November 1917 Balfour Declaration, issued by Foreign Secretary Arthur James Balfour to 2nd Baron Walter Rothschild, a leader of the British Jewish community, that stated the government's favorable view with respect to the establishment in of a Jewish state. The Balfour Declaration expressed that "His Majesty's Government view with favour the establishment in Palestine of a national home for the Jewish people."

B. Demise of the Ottoman Empire; The Balfour Declaration and Mandate Palestine

With the demise of the Ottoman Empire after World War I, Britain was confirmed as the League of Nations Mandatory Power in Palestine. Mandate Palestine was carved out of the defunct Ottoman Empire after World War I and placed under British administration from 1920 until the 1948 creation of Israel. The Council of the League of Nations issued its consent to Mandate Palestine on 24 July 1922, followed by the 16 September 1922 Transjordan Memorandum. The British Mandate of Palestine, a legal instrument that formalized British rule over Mandate Palestine, came into effect in 1923, following the ratification of the Treaty of Lausanne.

C. The Interwar Period

Between World War I and World War II, the Palestinians emerged out of the Ottoman Empire and immediately faced British control and a Zionist movement. Within this backdrop, the Palestinians went on strike in 1936. Growing unrest was complicated by Great Britain's conflicting obligations to both Jews (the 1917 Balfour Declaration) and Arab Nationalists (the 1915 Hussein/McMahon letters). While Zionists fully expected a Jewish state to be established in Palestine, the Arab Nationalists expected Palestine to become a Palestinian Arab nation.

This tension resulted in the 1936 British Peel Commission to investigate the situation, make recommendations and draw conclusions. The Commission concluded in 1937 that a Palestinian Arab/Zionist entente in Palestine to reconcile the contrary British obligations was not feasible. In light of this difficulty, it suggested partition.

Zionist leader Ben Gurion accepted the partition notion, but the Palestinian Arabs rejected it. After the Peel Commission report, sporadic violence broke out involving various paramilitary forces. Meanwhile, plans for a partition of Palestine continued at the international level.

D. General Assembly Resolution 181 (II): The UN Partition Plan for Palestine

1. Overview

On 29 November 1947, the UN GA adopted Resolution 181 (II), recommending the adoption and implementation of the Partition Plan for Palestine, a proposal that recommended a partition with economic union of Mandate Palestine to follow the termination of the British Mandate of Palestine. Resolution 181 (II) was pass with 33 nations in favor, 13 opposed and 10 abstentions.

The Palestinians and other Arabs challenged the UN's authority to partition Palestine and they argued that Palestine was to be included in the Arab territories that had been promised independence through an agreement with Great Britain in 1915 in exchange for Arab support in confronting the Ottomans and Germans in World War I. Despite Arab opposition, the Partition Plan passed. Fighting between Palestinians and Jews began upon the passing of the Partition Plan, eventually followed by the full-scale Arab-Israeli War after the British ended their Mandate of Palestine on 15 May 1948.

2.   Terms of the Partition Plan

The Partition Plan for Palestine allotted to Jews 55% of Palestine. The proposed Jewish state would have had a population of 499,000 Jews, and 438,000 Palestinians. Jerusalem was designated as a *corpus separatum* to be administered by the United Nations (*i.e.*, an international city).

PALESTINE
PLAN OF PARTITION
WITH ECONOMIC UNION
PROPOSED BY THE AD HOC COMMITTEE
ON THE PALESTINIAN QUESTION
PLAN DE PARTAGE
AVEC UNION ECONOMIQUE
PROPOSE PAR LA COMMISSION AD HOC
CHARGEE DE LA QUESTION PALESTINIENNE

Arab State   Etat arabe

Jewish State   Etat juif

City of   Ville de
Jerusalem   Jérusalem

Boundary
proposed
by UNSCOP

E. Palestine after the 1948 Arab-Israeli War

On the basis of Resolution 181 (II) of 1947, the British ended their Mandate of Palestine on 15 May 1948. The same day, Zionists declared statehood on the basis of the section of Resolution 181 (II) that called for a Jewish State (see ¶¶ 2-4, 7, etc.). By the time the 1949 Armistice was signed, Israel possessed 78% of Palestine in place of the original 55% envisioned by the Partition Plan.

F. 1967 Conquest and Occupation of Gaza, the West Bank and East Jerusalem

The remaining parts of Palestine, territories which were known in 1948 as Gaza and Eastern Palestine (including the unconquered part of Jerusalem) and are today known as the Gaza Strip, the West Bank and East Jerusalem, came under Egyptian and Jordanian control, with Egypt taking over Gaza administratively and Jordan taking over what remained of Jerusalem and the West Bank. Jordan eventually annexed them, which many Palestinians viewed as occupation. The UN also admonished Jordan for transforming East Jerusalem. The UN and the international community continued to recognize all of Jerusalem as defined by UN GA 181 (II) as an international *corpus separatum*. The majority of expelled Palestinians became refugees in Lebanon, Jordan, Syria, Iraq, Kuwait, Egypt, and in the remnants of Palestine, Gaza and the West Bank.

Israel conquered and occupied the remaining 22% of Palestine, the Syrian Golan Heights, and the Egyptian Sinai in the June 1967 war. UN Security Council Resolution 242 of 1967 called for Israel's withdrawal from the occupied territories, but Israel did not comply.

Eventually, the Sinai was returned to Egypt under security agreements. Jordan relinquished any claims to the West Bank and East Jerusalem in 1988 in a peace treaty with Israel in 1978. The West Bank and East Jerusalem became Palestinian territory under the responsibility of the Palestine Liberation Organization. In 1991, the Madrid/Oslo peace process was initiated based on acceptance by both parties of UN Security Council Resolution 242 of 1967. To date, however, the peace process between Israel and Palestine has been marked by a failed succession of attempted negotiations.

Chapter 2. The International Legal Refugee Framework

A. Introduction

1. Overview

After World War II, the international community was faced with the task of organizing thousands of displaced persons. There was a concerted effort to ensure that the atrocities committed during the war would never be repeated and part of this was achieved by adopting the Universal Declaration of Human Rights (**UDHR**) (1948). In order to secure the fundamental human rights of refugees, the Office of the UN High Commissioner for Refugees (**UNHCR**) was established in 1950. Headquartered in Geneva, Switzerland, the agency is mandated with the task of supervising international conventions providing for the protection of refugees. The main principle behind UNHCR and refugee law in general is to provide surrogate international protection for an individual where national protection of his fundamental rights has failed.

2. Applying for Refugee Status versus Asylee Status

UNHCR does not deal with the intake process of those who have already left their countries of residence. Such individuals may be welcomed by third party host states as asylees under local asylum laws. For example, the US permits any person who is already in the US or is entering the US to apply to remain in the US as an asylee. Under US law, the applicant must show that he has a reasonable fear of persecution because of race, religion, nationality, membership in a particular social group or political opinion, if forced to return to his country of last residence. Other States may apply a different set of criteria when evaluating whether to grant the right of asylum within its territory.

B. Convention Relating to the Status of Refugees

1. Introduction

a) *The UN High Commissioner for Refugees (1950) and the Refugee Convention (1951)*

(1) The UN High Commissioner for Refugees (1950)

UNHCR was established in 1950 by UN GA Resolution 428 (V) of 14 December 1950. Resolution 428 (V) adopted the Statute of UNHCR, which delineates the mandate of UNHCR as being (Art. 1 Annex Statute of UNHCR) (emphases added):

> providing international protection, under the auspices of the United Nations, to refugees who fall within the scope of the present Statute and of **seeking permanent solutions for the problem of refugees** by assisting governments and, subject to the approval of the governments concerned, private organizations to facilitate the **voluntary repatriation** of such refugees, or their **assimilation within new national communities**. In the exercise of his functions, more particularly when difficulties arise, and for instance with regard to any controversy concerning the international status of these persons, the High Commissioner shall request the opinion of an advisory committee on refugees if it is created.

The primary mission of UNHCR is thus to promote the protection of refugees by assisting governments and private partner organizations in seeking durable solutions for refugee problems. The role of UNHCR varies greatly from country to country, depending on several factors, including whether:

- there exists national legislation protecting the rights of refugees and national agencies or NGOs acting as refugee administrators;
- UNHCR is the primary refugee administrator or is even welcomed in the host country as an international presence.

While UNHCR does provide assistance and aid to refugees, its first priority is to advocate for the rights of refugees in host countries. It also encourages the development of national legislation that recognizes the rights of refugees and leads to a fair administration of those rights by national refugee agencies.

UNHCR may support refugees at the request of States or the UN itself.

(2) The Refugee Convention (1951)

In 1951 in Geneva, the United Nations Conference of Plenipotentiaries on the Status of Refugees and Stateless Persons convened under GA resolution 429 (V) of 14 December 1950. On 28 July 1951, the Conference of Plenipotentiaries approved the Convention Relating to the Status of Refugees (**Refugee Convention** or **CRSR**). The CRSR entered into force in 1954.

(3) Comparison

The CRSR is a legal instrument that lays out the human rights of refugees while UNHCR is an agency with a mandate to promote durable solutions to refugee crises. The CRSR is central to the activities of UNHCR by defining who is a refugee, setting out their rights and outlining the responsibilities of the international community in applying refugee protections.

b) *Refugee Protocol and States Party*

The CRSR was amended by the Protocol Relating to the Status of Refugees (**Refugee Protocol**) in 1967. With 148 States party to either the CRSR or the Refugee Protocol (145 are party to the CRSR and 3 are party to the Protocol only), the principles contained in the Convention and its Protocol now form part of customary international law.[1,2]

---

[1] Following are the 145 States party to the CRSR (which, in addition to the three States party to the 1967 Protocol only (Cape Verde, United States of America and Venezuela), make up a total of 148 States party to either the CRSR or the 1967 Protocol): Afghanistan, Albania, Algeria, Angola, Antigua and Barbuda, Argentina, Armenia, Australia, Austria, Azerbaijan, Bahamas, Belarus, Belgium, Belize, Benin, Bolivia (Plurinational State of), Bosnia and Herzegovina , Botswana, Brazil, Bulgaria, Burkina Faso, Burundi, Cambodia, Cameroon, Canada, Central African Republic, Chad, Chile, China , Colombia, Congo, Costa Rica, Côte d'Ivoire, Croatia , Cyprus, Czech Republic , Democratic Republic of the Congo, Denmark, Djibouti, Dominica, Dominican Republic, Ecuador, Egypt, El Salvador, Equatorial Guinea, Estonia, Ethiopia, Fiji, Finland, France, Gabon, Gambia, Georgia, Germany , , Ghana, Greece, Guatemala, Guinea, Guinea-Bissau, Haiti, Holy See, Honduras, Hungary, Iceland, Iran (Islamic Republic of), Ireland, Israel, Italy, Jamaica, Japan, Kazakhstan, Kenya, Kyrgyzstan, Latvia, Lesotho, Liberia,

Continued.../

2.   Defining "Refugee"

a)   Overview

Under Article 1 of the Convention, as modified by Article 1.2 of the Protocol, a refugee is any person who (Art. 1.A(2) CRSR):

> owing to well-founded fear of being persecuted for reasons of race, religion, nationality, membership of a particular social group or political opinion, is *outside the country of his nationality* and is unable, or owing to such fear, is unwilling to avail himself of the protection of that country; or who, not having a nationality and being outside the country of his former habitual residence as a result of such events, is unable or, owing to such fear, is unwilling to return to it.

There are thus three key elements to the definition of a "refugee" under the CRSR:

- The person must be *outside the country* of his nationality or habitual residence (*i.e.*, an international border must have been crossed);
- The reason for the person's displacement is a *well-founded fear of persecution*;
- The fear must be based on reasons of race, religion, nationality, membership of a particular social group or political opinion.

Liechtenstein, Lithuania, Luxembourg, Madagascar, Malawi, Mali, Malta, Mauritania, Mexico, Monaco, Montenegro, Morocco, Mozambique, Namibia, Nauru, Netherlands, New Zealand, Nicaragua, Niger, Nigeria, Norway, Panama, Papua New Guinea, Paraguay, Peru, Philippines, Poland, Portugal , Republic of Korea, Republic of Moldova, Romania, Russian Federation, Rwanda, Samoa, Sao Tome and Principe, Senegal, Serbia , Seychelles, Sierra Leone, Slovakia , Slovenia , Solomon Islands, Somalia, South Africa, Spain, St. Kitts and Nevis, St. Vincent and the Grenadines, Sudan, Suriname , Swaziland, Sweden, Switzerland, Tajikistan, The former Yugoslav Republic of Macedonia , Timor-Leste, Togo, Trinidad and Tobago, Tunisia, Turkey, Turkmenistan, Tuvalu , Uganda, Ukraine , United Kingdom of Great Britain and Northern Ireland, United Republic of Tanzania, Uruguay, Yemen, Zambia, Zimbabwe.
[2] Jordan, Lebanon and Syria, which hold some of the largest refugee populations in the world (mainly Palestinian, though more recently, Iraqi and Syrian), are among the States that are not party to the CRSR or its Protocol.

Several regional conventions have expanded this definition by including persons compelled to leave their country owing to generalized violence and aggression (*see, e.g.*, "Organization of African Unity Convention (1969)" and "Cartagena Declaration (1984)" under "Regional Conventions," *infra.*).

Article 1 also sets forth a series of exceptions to the general definition of "refugee" provided above. Even if there is a well-founded fear of persecution for reasons of race, religion, nationality, membership of a social group or political opinion, the following individuals may not seek refugee status:

- An individual who (1) has voluntarily re-availed himself of the protection of the country of his nationality; (2) having lost his nationality, has voluntarily reacquired it; (3) has acquired a new nationality and enjoys the protection of the country of his new nationality; (4) has voluntarily re-established himself in the country which he left or outside which he remained owing to fear of persecution; or (5) can no longer, because the circumstances in connection with which he has been recognized as a refugee have ceased to exist, continue to refuse to avail himself of the protection of the country of his nationality or is able to return to the country of his former habitual residence (Art. 1.C CRSR);
- Persons who are at present receiving from organs or agencies of the UN other than UNHCR protection or assistance (Art. 1.D CRSR);
- A person who is recognized by the competent authorities of the country in which he has taken residence as having the rights and obligations which are attached to the possession of the nationality of that country (Art. 1.E CRSR);
- Any person with respect to whom there are serious reasons for considering that: (a) he has committed a crime against peace, a war crime, or a crime against humanity; (b) he has committed a serious non-political crime outside the country of refuge prior to his admission to that country as a refugee; or (c) he has been guilty of acts contrary to the purposes and principles of the UN (Art. 1.F CRSR).

b) Refugees versus Internally Displaced Persons

Internally displaced persons (**IDPs**) are individuals who have had to leave their homes due to persecution, but who are still within their countries of residence. Because they have never crossed an international border, they cannot be considered to be "refugees."

Nonetheless, UNHCR has a mandate to work with IDPs. No treaty governs the protections to be afforded by IDPs, but some guidelines on their treatment and protection exist.

3. Refugee Rights

a) Overview

The CRSR defines the rights of individuals who are granted asylum and the responsibilities of nations that grant asylum. The basic principle under the Convention is that refugees should be granted no less favorable treatment than similarly situated foreign residents under the law of their host countries.

b) Refugee Rights

The CRSR is in many ways a human rights convention in that it seeks to provide protection in the form of securing refugees' human rights. The CRSR provides such persons the right of asylum in States party to the CRSR as well as a host of other rights. States party to the Convention are obliged to guarantee the following refugee rights, among others:

- Intellectual property rights, including copyrights, patents and trademarks, that are accorded in refugees' countries of habitual residence (Art. 14 CRSR);
- Right of association (Art. 15 CRSR);
- Access to courts (Art. 16. CRSR);
- Favorable conditions for gainful wage-earning and self-employment and for the practice of the liberal professions (Arts. 17, 19 CRSR);
- Welfare, including housing (Art. 21 CRSR), public education (Art. 22 CRSR) and access to public relief and assistance (Art. 23 CRSR).

c) Obligations of States Party

States party to the CRSR are under the following duties, among others:

- Prohibition of discrimination as to the admission of refugees on the basis of race, religion, or country of origin;

- Prohibition of expulsion or return (the principle of "*non-refoulement*") (Art. 33 CRSR);
- Cooperation "with the Office of the United Nations High Commissioner for Refugees, or any other agency of the United Nations which may succeed it, in the exercise of its functions and shall in particular facilitate its duty of supervising the application of the provisions of [the] Convention" (Art. 35 CRSR);
- Communication "to the Secretary-General of the United Nations the laws and regulations which they may adopt to ensure the application of [the] Convention" (Art. 36 CRSR).

4.   Refugees Unlawfully Residing in their Country of Refuge

It is not necessary for individuals claiming refugee status to lawfully enter the State where they make their refugee claim: "The Contracting States shall not impose penalties, on account of their illegal entry or presence, on refugees who, coming directly from a territory where their life or freedom was threatened ... enter or are present in their territory without authorization, provided they present themselves without delay to the authorities and show good cause for their illegal entry or presence" (Art. 31(1) CRSR).

5.   *Principle of Non-Refoulement*

a)   *General Rule and Application*

While refugees are entitled to the same basic human rights as everyone else, the particular right held by refugees is the right of *non-refoulement*. The principle of *non-refoulement* is a non-derogable right that grants refugees protection against forcible return to territories where their life or freedom would be in danger. This principle places an absolute obligation on States party not to return refugees to countries in which their lives or freedom would be in danger. The CRSR states that "no Contracting State shall expel or return ("refouler") a refugee in any manner whatsoever to the frontiers of territories where his life or freedom would be threatened on account of his race, religion, nationality, membership of a particular social group or political opinion" (Art. 33(1) CRSR). Because the treaty applies in situations where the individual's "life or freedom *would be* threatened" (emphasis added), the standard is an objective one that does not take into account the individual's perception as to whether his life or liberty would be threatened.

In practice, this means that once a refugee arrives at immigration control at an airport or seaport to claim refugee status, he should not be turned away. Nor should he be required to leave while his application is pending, provided he makes a *prima facie* claim.

The principle of *non-refoulement* is violated when any one of the following three elements is met:

- Asylum seekers are rejected at a border when they have no possibility of obtaining asylum elsewhere;
- Refugees are deported from their country of asylum to a territory where their life, liberty or physical security may be in danger; or
- Refugees are forcibly returned to their country of origin where they fear persecution or are sent to a third party country whence they may be deported to their country of origin.

b) Exceptions

The principle of *non-refoulement* is widely accepted as a part of customary international law that is binding even on States not party to the CRSR. However, there are exceptions to its practice. *Non-refoulement* does not apply when there are "reasonable grounds for regarding as a danger to the security" of the State of refuge, or when the refugee has "been convicted by a final judgment of a particularly serious crime [and] constitutes a danger to the community of that country" (Art. 33(2) CRSR). The refugee may also be expelled from the State of refuge "on grounds of national security or public order" (Art. 32.1 CRSR). However, the State of refuge may be inhibited by practicing this right if relevant provisions to another treaty to which it is a party apply. For example, under Article 3 of the Convention against Torture and Other Cruel, Inhuman or Degrading Treatment (1984), the State may be prevented from returning the person to another State if there are grounds to believe that he would be in danger of torture.

C. The Refugee Framework

1. Definition of "Refugee Protection"

a) Traditional Definition: Advocating for Durable Solutions

The CRSR does not provide a definition of "protection" with respect to its interventions on behalf of refugees in the same what that it provides a definition of "refugee." The UNHCR Statute does, however, define the protection that falls under the competence of the High Commissioner. It states as follows (¶8 UNHCR Statute):

> The High Commissioner shall provide for the protection of refugees falling under the competence of his Office by:
> (a) Promoting the conclusion and ratification of international conventions for the protection of refugees, supervising their application and proposing amendments thereto;
> ...
> (c) Assisting governmental and private efforts to promote *voluntary repatriation* or *assimilation* within new national communities;
> (d) Promoting the admission of refugees, not excluding those in the most destitute categories, to the territories of States;
> (e) Endeavouring to obtain permission for refugees to transfer their assets and especially those necessary for their *resettlement*;

Paragraph 8 of the UNHCR Statute thus highlights the three traditional durable solutions that should be made available to refugees: repatriation, assimilation (local integration) and resettlement to third party countries.

b) Expanded Definition: Advocating for Durable Solutions as well as Providing Assistance

According to UNHCR, its "international protection function, as derived from its Statutes and the 1951 Convention relating to the Status of Refugees, has evolved steadily over the past five decades. It began almost as a surrogate for consular and diplomatic protection and has now expanded to include ensuring the basic rights of refugees and their physical safety and security." Thus, for UNHCR, "refugee protection" covers the full gamut of activities through which refugees' rights are secured, including not only advocacy in the search for durable solutions but also assistance in the sense of providing for basic needs. This is further made clear by the working definition of protection adopted by the UNHCR Department of International Protection, which holds that protection including not only realizing the right to assistance, but also implementing durable solutions. In its Checklist for UNHCR Staff, UNHCR holds that protection:

> encompasses all activities aimed at ensuring the enjoyment, on equal terms of the rights of women, men, girls and boys of concern to UNHCR in accordance with the letter and spirit of the relevant bodies of law [including] interventions by States or UNHCR on behalf of asylum-seekers and refugees to ensure that their rights, security, and welfare are recognized and safeguarded in accordance with international standards. Such interventions will, amongst others, be deemed to: ensuring respect for the principle of *non-refoulement*; promoting admission to safety and access to fair procedures for the determination of refugee status; upholding humane standards of treatment; *realizing the right to assistance and services*; promoting non-discrimination, and the implementation of *durable solutions* (Designing Protection Strategies and Measuring Progress: Checklist for UNHCR Staff, Department of International Protection, UNHCR, 2002).

Thus, under UNHCR's expanded definition, protection includes the full gamut of activities through which refugees' rights may be secured. Such activities may include assistance, but protection is not necessarily limited to assistance and may comprise other activities, such as the implementation of durable solutions.

2. Durable Solutions

The international refugee legal framework provides refugees with three traditional durable solutions, which in principle are subject to the choice of refugees on the basis of the principle of voluntariness.

a) *Voluntary Repatriation (to the First Country)*

While it is not always possible, the solution most often preferred is voluntary repatriation. This solution involves the return of the refugee to the country of origin once the threat to freedom and safety has been eliminated. Repatriation must be a voluntary decision by the refugee. It is the responsibility of the international community to provide the refugee with clear and accurate information regarding the situation in their country of origin.

b) Local Integration (in the Second Country)

The refugee framework's second durable solution is local integration, whereby a host nation adjacent to a refugee-producing country absorbs the refugee population into its own population. Local integration in the host nation remains one of the primary durable solutions, but host nations are under no obligation to absorb refugee populations. If they do, refugees are granted the full rights of foreign residents and are assimilated into the local community with access to jobs, education, health care and basic services. If host nations are unable or unwilling to integrate refugees into their societies, then the refugees normally wind up living in refugee camps or living illegally in urban centers until another durable solution becomes available.

c) Resettlement (to a Third Country)

Resettlement is a means by which several countries can share the responsibility of protecting refugees, rather than placing the entire burden on countries adjacent to refugee-producing nations. There are seventeen countries with resettlement programs: Argentina, Australia, Benin, Brazil, Burkina Faso, Canada, Chile, Denmark, Finland, Iceland, Ireland, Netherlands, New Zealand, Norway, Sweden, the United Kingdom and the United States. The resettlement programs move refugees from a host nation to a third nation where they are granted permanent residence.

Each nation with a resettlement program sets the conditions for resettlement and the number of refugees that it accepts annually. For example, in 2011, the US accepted approximately 75,000 refugees, about half of which were from the Middle East, and many of these Iraqi refugees were displaced in the Iraq War and will return to Iraq when the situation stabilizes. In the US, as in many other countries with resettlement programs, the number of refugees accepted changes on an annual basis.

3.   Temporary Settlements for Refugees

Refugee camps are a significant component of the refugee regime. In the camps, refugees are identified and registered and wait for a "durable solution" to materialize. Humanitarian aid earmarked for refugees is distributed in the camps, which become a means of serving the refugees with educational services, health care, food, water and temporary shelter, all while maintaining control of the population until a long-term solution is identified.

Many refugees do not like the confinement of the camps and choose to move to the urban centers of the host nation. This presents many challenges, both for refugees and for the refugee administration. Urban refugees tend to move more often, making it difficult for refugee agency caseworkers to keep track of them. They are also vulnerable in urban settings because they may be mistaken by local authorities as illegal immigrants as opposed to refugees with a right to employment. Urban refugees often settle in areas with limited access to education, health services and low quality housing and may need to address hostility from urban residents who do not distinguish them from growing numbers of unwelcome economic migrants.

4.   Refugee Administrative System Partners

a)   *National Agencies*

UNHCR's goal is that each nation would have national legislation, agencies and procedures to address refugees and administer refugee protections. Such institutions comprise the last element of the refugee framework.

For many countries, the agency that addresses refugee status determination and administration is the same agency that handles immigration. Such agencies are normally located within a ministry of foreign affairs. In the US, the agency is the United States Citizenship and Immigration Services (**USCIS**), a component of the United States Department of Homeland Security (**DHS**). As is the case of many nations, USCIS processes not only asylum and refugee applications, but also immigrant visa petitions and naturalization petitions.

b) Non-Governmental Organizations

When a country has an immigration office, but no national legislation, agencies or procedures to address local refugees, UNHCR will often step in as the primary agency of refugee administration. When a country has such legislation or agencies in place, UNHCR often works in a supportive role in tandem with national agencies.

In both cases, NGOs often play a role in refugee administration and fill the gaps between UNHCR and national agencies. NGOs may work in any of the following areas:

- distribution of services;
- refugee status determination (**RSD**); or
- advocacy for legislating refugee protections.

Together with national agencies, NGOs may participate in complete or partial refugee administration, parallel to that of UNHCR.

Chapter 3. The Place of UNRWA within the Global Refugee Framework

A. Introduction

Prior to the establishment of UNHCR, the United Nations Relief and Works Agency for Palestine Refugees in the Near East (**UNRWA**) was established as a UN GA subsidiary organ by GA Resolution 302 (IV) of 1949 to provide assistance and protection through relief and jobs to 652,000 Arabs who fled or were expelled from Israel during the Arab-Israeli War. Today, UNRWA provides assistance to some five million Palestinian refugees living in the West Bank, the Gaza Strip, Jordan, Lebanon and Syria to achieve their full potential in human development, pending a just and durable solution to their plight.

UNRWA's services encompass the following forms of assistance:

- health care;
- education;
- social services and job provision (in public works projects);
- camp infrastructure and improvement;
- microfinance; and
- emergency assistance[3]

With over 32,000 staff, UNRWA is the largest UN organization. The overwhelming majority of UNRWA staff (more than 30,000) are locally-filled by Palestinians, thus fulfilling the organization's mandate to provide jobs as well as relief services.

---

[3] For example, a Psycho-Social Support Program launched by UNRWA as part of its emergency operations in the oPt in 2000, after the start of the Second Intifada.

What first strikes the casual observer is the presence of permanent structures at the UNRWA camps, which replaced the tents that Palestinian refugees originally lived in with more durable shelters.

B. Mandate: Assistance and Protection until a Durable Solution is Available

1.   Under Resolution 302 (IV): "Direct Relief and Works Programmes"

In 1949, after the creation of UNCCP, UN GA Resolution 302 (IV) established UNRWA in order (¶ 7):

> (a) To carry out in collaboration with local governments the *direct relief and works programmes* as recommended by the Economic Survey Mission [of the UNCCP];
>
> (b) To consult with the interested Near Eastern Governments concerning measures to be taken by them *preparatory to the time when international assistance for relief and works projects is no longer available.*

UNRWA is thus mandated to provide protection and assistance for Palestinian refugees, who are operationally defined by UNRWA as "persons whose normal place of residence was Palestine between June 1946 and May 1948, who lost their homes and livelihood as a result of the 1948 Arab-Israeli conflict." This definition also includes the decedents of those identified as Palestinian refugees. UNRWA consequently has a very narrow and distinct mandate when compared to UNHCR.

Unlike Resolution 194 (III) of 1948, which established the UNCCP and references repatriation and resettlement as durable solutions to the Palestinian refugee problem,[4] Resolution 302 (IV) of 1949 does not discuss durable solutions. Under its mandate, UNRWA takes no position on or deal with durable solutions. Its mandate is strictly to provide direct relief and works programs to Palestinian refugees until a durable solution to the Israel-Palestine conflict is reached.

2.   Expanded Reading of Resolution 302 (IV) to Include Protection

a)   Overview

UNRWA's mandate cannot be seen to be limited to the language provided in Resolution 302 (IV) of 1949, which does not set out to adopt a "statute" for UNRWA but rather provides general guidelines and requests for the Agency. UNRWA's mandate must instead be read according to Resolution 302 (IV) in conjunction with the other resolutions of the UN GA that have expanded UNRWA's mandate to assist persons displaced by the "1967 and subsequent hostilities," as well as with requests from other UN organs, including the Secretariat acting through the Secretary-General, to expand UNRWA's mandate. These Resolutions and requests of the UN Secretary General form the basis of an expansion of the Resolution 302 (IV) UNRWA mandate to include various activities that fall within "protection," as defined by the Inter-Agency Standing Committee (**IASC**) as (IASC, *Growing the Sheltering Tree: Protecting Rights through Humanitarian Action*, Sept. 2002, 11):

> all activities aimed at obtaining full respect for the rights of the individual in accordance with the letter and spirit of the relevant

---

[4] Resolution 194 (III) of 1948 instructs the UNCCP to "facilitate the repatriation, resettlement and economic and social rehabilitation of the refugees and the payment of compensation" (¶ 11).

bodies of law (that is, human rights law, international humanitarian law, refugee law)."[5]

On this basis, UNRWA legal advisor Surya Sinha advocates viewing UNRWA's mandate "pragmatically and not as something cast in immutable terms 40 years ago" (Benjamin Schiff, *Refugees Unto the Third Generation, UN Aid to Palestinians* (Syracuse University Press, 1995), p. 252). UNRWA's undertaking of protection work in addition to direct relief and works programs has been based on a flexible approach to its humanitarian mandate in response to requests of the international community. In the words of UNRWA ("UNRWA and the Transitional Period: a Five-Year Perspective on the Role of the Agency and its Financial Requirements," p. 5):

> An analysis of resolutions adopted on UNRWA by the General Assembly since 1949 shows that there has been no rigid or restrictive definition of the Agency's mandate. Rather, there has been an inclination to request UNRWA to take on broader responsibilities, either with regard to programmes or with regard to beneficiaries, in response to periodic emergencies in the region.

b) *Expanded Reading on the Basis of Requests of the International Community*

UNRWA's mandate must be read according to Resolution 302 (IV), which provides general guidelines but does not does not elaborate a "statute" for the Agency, in conjunction with the other resolutions of the UN GA, requests by the international community for UNRWA to act and changing circumstances and emergency needs, as detailed further below.

(1) Facilitation of Refugees' Resettlements to Iraq and Libya (1950s)

In the 1950s, for example, UNRWA facilitated some small-scale resettlements through a Placement Services Office that offered loans

---

[5] Note: This section does not take into account the definition of "protection" that falls under the competence of the High Commissioner under the UHCHR Statute, which in ¶8 highlights the three traditional durable solutions that should be made available to refugees: repatriation, assimilation (local integration) and resettlement to third party countries.

and other assistance to Palestinian refugees seeking to resettle in Iraq or Libya (30 June 1952, "Report of the Commissioner-General of the United Nations Relief and Works Agency for Palestine Refugees in the Near East," UN Doc. A/2171).

(2) Secretary General's Request for Protection During the First Intifada (1987-1993)

For example, during the First Intifada (1987-1993), the UN Secretary General suggested that additional international staff be placed in the West Bank and Gaza Strip to provide "general assistance" or the type of protection in which "an outside agency intervenes with the authorities of the occupying Power to help individuals or groups of individuals to resist violations of their rights ... and to cope with the day-to-day difficulties of life under occupation" (UN Doc. S/19443, 10). UNRWA responded through the Refugee Affairs Officer (**RAO**) program, which from 1988 to 1996 provided basic protection by defusing tensions during confrontations between the IDF and Palestinian refugees and helping to ensure refugees' access to emergency aid.

(3) Establishment of a Senior Protection Policy Adviser Post (Resolution 62/236 of 2007)

UN GA Resolution 62/236 of 2007 approved funding through the UN regular budget the establishment of an additional senior post for an UNRWA Senior Protection Policy Adviser, thus further confirming UNRWA's protection mandate.

(4) Protection Work Affirmed by UN General Assembly (Resolutions 63/92 and 63/93 of 2008)

The Agency's protection mandate is further exemplified in UN GA Resolution 63/93 of 2008, where the GA restated that it was aware of "the valuable work done by the Agency in providing protection to the Palestinian people, in particular, Palestine refugees".

In addition to Resolution 63/93, Resolution 63/92, also of 2008, expands UNRWA's mandate to assist persons displaced by the "1967 and subsequent hostilities."

C. Applicable Laws

1.   Employment Regulations and Rules

a) Overview

UNRWA international staff (in the professional and general service categories) are governed by the International Staff Regulations, Cod./I/61/Rev. 3/Amend.48, dated 1 March 1992, and the International Staff Rules, Cod./I/61/Rev.4, dated 1 May 2002.

UNRWA area post staff are governed by the Area Staff Regulations, Cod./A/59/Rev.25, of January 1988, and the Area Staff Rules, also Cod./A/59/Rev.25, of January 1988.

b) Disciplinary Measures

The Commissioner-General may establish administrative machinery that will be available to advise the Commissioner-General in disciplinary cases (Regulation I0.1 International Staff Regulations).

c) Appeals

(1) Overview

Under Regulation 11.1 of the International Staff Regulations, the Commissioner-General is to establish administrative machinery to advise him in case of any appeal by staff members:

- against an administrative decision alleging the non-observance of their terms of appointment (or of any pertinent regulations and rules); or
- against disciplinary action.

(2) United Nations Administrative Tribunal and United Nations Appeals Tribunal

Under Regulation 11.2 of the International Staff Regulations, the UN Administrative Tribunal was to hear and pass judgment upon applications from staff members alleging non-observance of their terms of appointment (including all pertinent regulations and rules). However, 30 June 2009 marked the end of the mandate of the United Nations

Administrative Tribunal, which was replaced by the United Nations Appeals Tribunal (UNAT) from 1 July 2009 onwards.

(3) Current UNRWA Appeals Framework

At present, a staff member alleging non-observance of terms of appointment (including all pertinent regulations and rules) may:

- File an application to the UNRWA Dispute Tribunal;
- Appeal a decision of the UNRWA Dispute Tribunal to the United Nations Appeals Tribunal, the court of second instance within the UN internal justice system, which hears cases in which a lower court errs on questions of fact, procedure or law.

2. Immunity

a) Overview

Sovereign States are generally immune from legal jurisdiction and thus cannot be civilly sued or criminally prosecuted. This is based on the old adage, "the king can do no wrong," taken from the common law tradition. However, States may waive part or all of this immunity by consenting to be sued or prosecuted in certain cases. This is normally done through the approval of statutes that recognize causes of action that may be brought in the State's courts to try the sovereign for some alleged wrong attributable to the sovereign.

b) Restrictive State Immunity

Whether or not States have partially waived sovereign immunity through statutes that recognize causes of action that may be brought against them, many States recognize the doctrine of *restrictive state immunity*, where a State may be sued when it has engaged in a purely commercial transaction. This doctrine emerged during the early twentieth century, in response to increased participation of state governments in international trade.

c) Convention on the Privileges and Immunities of the United Nations (1946)

(1) Overview

Article 105 of the UN Charter states that the UN "shall enjoy in the territory of each of its Members such privileges and immunities as are necessary for the fulfilment of its purposes." These privileges and immunities are extended to "Representatives of the Members of the United Nations and officials of the Organization ... for the independent exercise of their functions in connexion with the Organization" (Art. 105 CUN). Article 105 goes on to state that the GA may may "recommendations with a view to determining the details of the application of [these privileges and immunities] or may propose conventions to the Members of the United Nations for this purpose" (Art. 105 CUN).

Within this context, the UN GA adopted the 1946 Convention on the Privileges and Immunities of the United Nations and the 1947 Convention on Privileges and Immunities of the Specialized Agencies.

Just as the VCDR grants diplomatic mission staff privileges and immunities, the Convention on the Privileges and Immunities of the United Nations (**CPIUN**), passed by the GA on 13 February 1946, grants UN mission staff the privileges and immunities necessary for them to carry out their work. It requires UN member States to grant privileges and immunities to the UN, its assets and officials. As of August 2013, it has been ratified by 160 of the 193 UN member States.[6]

---

[6] Following are the 160 States party to the CPIUN: Afghanistan, Albania, Algeria, Angola, Antigua and Barbuda, Argentina, Armenia, Australia, Austria, Azerbaijan, Bahamas, Bahrain, Bangladesh, Barbados, Belarus, Belgium, Belize, Bolivia (Plurinational State of), Bosnia and Herzegovina, Brazil, Brunei Darussalam, Bulgaria, Burkina Faso, Burundi, Cambodia, Cameroon, Canada, Central African Republic, Chile, China, Colombia, Congo, Costa Rica, Côte d'Ivoire, Croatia, Cuba, Cyprus, Czech Republic, Democratic Republic of the Congo, Denmark, Djibouti, Dominica, Dominican Republic, Ecuador, Egypt, El Salvador, Estonia, Ethiopia, Fiji, Finland, France, Gabon, Gambia, Georgia, Germany, Ghana, Greece, Guatemala, Guinea, Guyana, Haiti, Honduras, Hungary, Iceland, India, Indonesia, Iran (Islamic Republic of), Iraq, Ireland, *Israel*, Italy, Jamaica, Japan, *Jordan*, Kazakhstan, Kenya, Kuwait, Kyrgyzstan, Lao People's Democratic Republic, Latvia, *Lebanon*, Lesotho, Liberia, Libya, Liechtenstein, Lithuania, Luxembourg, Madagascar, Malawi, Malaysia, Mali, Malta, Mauritius, Mexico, Micronesia (Federated States of), Monaco, Mongolia, Montenegro, Morocco,

Continued.../

(2) Privileges and Immunities Granted to the United Nations and Its Personnel

(a) Juridical Personality (Art. I CPIUN)

The CPIUN begins by extending to the UN juridical personality with the capacity to: (a) contract; (b) acquire and dispose of immovable and movable property; and (c) institute legal proceedings (Art. I, § 1 CPIUN).

(b) Property and Assets (Art. II CPIUN)

The CPIUN then discusses a series of provisions relating to UN property and assets, which are immune from:

- "[L]egal process except insofar as in any particular case it has expressly waived its immunity" (Art. II, §§ 2 CPIUN);
- "[S]earch, requisition, confiscation, expropriation and any other form of interference" (Art. II, § 3 CPIUN); and
- Direct taxes (excluding public utility services); customs duties and prohibitions and restrictions on imports and exports in respect of articles imported or exported for official UN use and of UN publications (Art. II, § 7 CPIUN).

(c) Diplomatic Communications (Art. III CPIUN)

The CPIUN extends diplomatic immunity to UN official communications, which are to enjoy treatment not less favorable than that that accorded to "to any other Government including its diplomatic mission" (Art. III, § 9 CPIUN) and to correspondence by courier or in bags (the diplomatic bag or pouch), which "shall have the same

---

Mozambique, Myanmar, Namibia, Nepal, Netherlands, New Zealand, Nicaragua, Niger, Nigeria, Norway, Pakistan, Panama, Papua New Guinea, Paraguay, Peru, Philippines, Poland, Portugal, Qatar, Republic of Korea, Republic of Moldova, Romania, Russian Federation, Rwanda, San Marino, Senegal, Serbia, Seychelles, Sierra Leone, Singapore, Slovakia, Slovenia, Somalia, South Africa, Spain, Sri Lanka, St. Lucia, Sudan, Sweden, Switzerland, **Syrian Arab Republic**, Tajikistan, Thailand, The former Yugoslav Republic of Macedonia, Togo, Trinidad and Tobago, Tunisia, Turkey, Turkmenistan, Uganda, Ukraine, United Arab Emirates, United Kingdom of Great Britain and Northern Ireland, United Republic of Tanzania, United States of America, Uruguay, Venezuela (Bolivarian Republic of), Viet Nam, Yemen, Zambia, Zimbabwe.

immunities and privileges as diplomatic couriers and bags" (Art. III, § 10 CPIUN).

(d) Representatives of UN Members, Officials and Experts (Arts. IV-VI CPIUN)

Functional immunity is extended to:

- Representatives (or delegates) of UN member States to the principal and subsidiary UN organs and to UN conferences (Art. IV CPIUN);
- Officials, whose categories are to be specified by the Secretary-General. They are immune from legal process in respect of words spoken or written and acts performed in their official capacity, are exempt from taxation with respect to their UN salaries and may import duty-free furniture and effects at the time of first taking up their post in the country in question (Art. V, § 18 CPIUN). These rights may be waived by the Secretary-General if immunity would impede the course of justice (Art. V, § 20 CPIUN); and
- Experts performing missions for the UN, where such privileges and immunities are necessary for the independent exercise of their functions during the period of their missions (Art. VI, § 22 CPIUN).

(e) Laissez-Passer (Art. VII CPIUN)

States must recognize *laissez-passers* issued by the UN to its officials and must accept them as valid travel documents (Art. VII, § 24 CPIUN).

(f) Dispute Settlement (Art. VIII CPIUN)

Modes of settlement of disputes arising out disputes of a private character, including contracts, to which the UN is a party, and those involving UN officials enjoying immunity are subject to the provisions made by the UN to settle the same (Art. VIII, § 29 CPIUN).

Chapter 4. Human Rights Instruments Applicable to Refugees

A. General Overview

1. Introduction

Like all other human beings, refugees enjoy the basic human rights described in various international legal instruments, including regional and international treaties and declarations). Refugees are thus the subject of not only treaties that deal directly with refugee questions, such as the CRSR and Refugee Protocol, but also of international law dealing with human rights protections. The most important of these texts are summarized below.

2. Sources of International Human Rights Law

a) Non-Binding International Declarations

(1) Universal Declaration of Human Rights (UN 1948)

The UDHR was adopted by the UN General Assembly on 10 December 1948. Most sources consider the UDHR to be a nonbinding resolution that set forth a "common standard of achievement for all peoples and all nations" (Preamble UDHR). Other sources view it as an elaboration of the human rights provisions of the UN Charter and thus claim that it is binding through the Charter. Yet others consider it to be a source of binding customary international law.

Some commentators argue that Art. 13.2 of the UDHR is of particular relevance to the Palestinian refugees. It provides: "Everyone has the right to leave any country, including his own, and to return to his country."

The UDHR was passed by a vote of 48 in favor, zero against and eight abstentions (Byelorussian SSR, Czechoslovakia, Poland, Ukrainian

SSR, USSR, Yugoslavia, South Africa and Saudi Arabia). The following countries voted in favor of the Declaration: Afghanistan, Argentina, Australia, Belgium, Bolivia, Brazil, Burma, Canada, Chile, China, Colombia, Costa Rica, Cuba, Denmark, the Dominican Republic, Ecuador, Egypt, El Salvador, Ethiopia, France, Greece, Guatemala, Haiti, Iceland, India, Iran, Iraq, Lebanon, Liberia, Luxembourg, Mexico, Netherlands, New Zealand, Nicaragua, Norway, Pakistan, Panama, Paraguay, Peru, Philippines, Thailand, Sweden, Syria, Turkey, United Kingdom, United States, Uruguay and Venezuela.

(2) Cairo Declaration on Human Rights in Islam (1990)

The Cairo Declaration on Human Rights in Islam (**CDHRI**) is a declaration of the member States of the Organisation of Islamic Cooperation (**OIC**) (known as the Organisation of the Islamic Conference prior to 28 June 2011) adopted in Cairo in 1990, which provides an overview on the Islamic perspective on human rights and affirms *Shari'a* as its sole source. The purpose of the CDHRI is "general guidance for Member States [of the OIC] in the Field of human rights." This declaration is usually seen as an Islamic response to the UDHR of 1948.

b) Customary International Law

Customary international law may be defined according to the following three elements: (i) a consistent and recurrent state practice; (ii) developed over time; that is (iii) undertaken out of a sense of legal obligation. In this manner, the Restatement 3d of the Foreign Relations Law of the US defines customary international law as resulting "from a general and consistent practice of States followed by them from a sense of legal obligation" (§ 102(2) RFR). This general and consistent practice is often referred to as "state practice." As the ICJ has declared in the Libya/Malta case (1985), this state practice, together with the *opinio juris* of States, forms the substance of customary law.

Customary international law in the field of human rights develops primarily as a result of international treaties that are adopted by a large plurality of States, such that the practices contained therein become general and consistent binding practices in the international arena, as well as when international declarations are widely accepted and practiced by the international community. Some have argued, for example, that the UDHR, though it is a non-binding declaration, has to some extent evolved into a source of binding customary international law because of its wide acceptance and consistent and recurrent practice by States.

c) Binding International Treaties and Conventions

(1) United Nations Treaties

(a) United Nations Charter (1945)

The CUN states that one of the purposes of the UN is to achieve "international co-operation in ... promoting and encouraging respect for human rights and for fundamental freedoms for all without distinction as to race, sex, language, or religion" (Art. 1.3 CUN). This is reemphasized in Article 55, which declares that "the United Nations shall promote ... universal respect for and observance of, human rights and fundamental freedoms for all without distinction as to race, sex, language, or religion" (Art. 55 CUN). The fact that nondiscrimination is the one right that is expressly mentioned in the CUN ("distinction as to race, sex, language, or religion") indicates the extent to which States party took this right seriously.

(b) Convention on the Prevention and Punishment of the Crime of Genocide (1948)

The Convention on the Prevention and Punishment of the Crime of Genocide (Genocide Convention) (**CPPG**) was adopted by the UN General Assembly on 9 December 1948, just one day before the adoption of the Universal Declaration of Human Rights. The Convention, which entered into force in 1951, defines genocide in its second Article as:

> any of the following acts committed with intent to destroy, in whole or in part, a national, ethnical, racial or religious group, as such:
> (a) Killing members of the group;
> (b) Causing serious bodily or mental harm to members of the group;

(c) Deliberately inflicting on the group conditions of life calculated to bring about its physical destruction in whole or in part;

(d) Imposing measures intended to prevent births within the group;

(e) Forcibly transferring children of the group to another group.

It is important to note that under this definition, the application of the Genocide Convention is not predicated on the existence of an armed conflict.

The Genocide Convention is an example of a human rights instrument that creates an affirmative duty to act. It requires not only that its 140 States party refrain from the crime of genocide, but also that they "undertake to prevent and to punish" genocide (Art. I CPPG) and further pledge "to grant extradition in accordance with their laws and treaties in force" of persons charged with genocide (Art. VII CPPG). The ICJ thus found in the Bosnian Genocide Case (*Bosnia and Herzegovina v. Serbia and Montenegro*) (2007) that Belgrade breached international law by failing to prevent the 1995 genocide in the town of Srebrenica (of the political entity Republika Srpska, within Bosnia and Herzegovina) and for failing to try or transfer to the ICTY those accused of genocide, thus violating its obligations under the Genocide Conventions.

(c) The International Covenant on Civil and Political Rights (1966) and the International Covenant on Economic, Social and Cultural Rights (1966)

(i) *Overview and Comparison*

The ICCPR and the ICESCR are two international treaties that aimed at converting the nonbinding provisions of the UDHR into binding treaty provisions. Together with the UDHR, the ICCPR and ICESCR have come to constitute the so-called "International Bill of Rights."

Because the USSR and US were unable to agree as to the rights that should be enumerated (the US argued that economic and social rights do not exist, while the USSR wished to codify them), two separate treaties resulted. Unlike the UDHR, which took only a few years to draft because it was not binding, the drafting of the ICCPR and the ICESCR took eighteen years.

Unlike the ICESCR, which the US signed but did not ratify, the ICCPR was signed and ratified by both the US and the USSR. The ICCPR has 154 States party, while the ICESCR has 151.

(ii) *International Covenant on Civil and Political Rights (ICCPR)*

(a) *Overview*

States party to the ICCPR, which came into effect on 23 March 1976, undertake to protect the wide range of civil and political rights, including a right to life (Art. 6 ICCPR), prohibitions on torture (Art. 7 ICCPR) and slavery (Art. 8 ICCPR), prohibitions on arbitrary arrest or detention (Art. 9.1 ICCPR), a right to trial within a reasonable time of arrest or detainment (Art. 9.3 ICCPR) and to freedom of thought, conscience and religion (Art. 18 ICCPR), as well as freedom of expression (Art. 19 ICCPR).

The ICCPR requires States not only to agree to not violate these rights, but also to ensure the rights by protecting them from other member States' violations (Art. 2(3) ICCPR). It thus incorporates an affirmative duty to act.

(b) *Right to Return One's Country*

Some commentators hold that Art. 12.4 of the ICCPR is of particular relevance to the Palestinian refugees. It provides: "No one shall be arbitrarily deprived of the right to enter his own country."

(c) *States Party*

The majority of States in the international community are parties to the ICCPR. As of April 2011, there were seventy two signatories and 167 parties. The following States have signed but have not yet ratified the Convention: the People's Republic of China, Comoros, Cuba, Nauru and São Tomé and Príncipe. The following States have neither signed nor ratified the ICCPR: Antigua and Barbuda, Bhutan, Brunei, Burma (Myanmar), Fiji, Kiribati, Malaysia, Marshall Islands, Micronesia, Oman, Palau, Qatar, Saint Kitts and Nevis, Saint Lucia, Saudi Arabia, Singapore, Solomon Islands, Tonga, Tuvalu, United Arab Emirates and Vatican City.

(d) Optional Protocol

Because there are no specified enforcement mechanisms in the ICCPR, States party drafted an optional protocol that allows for complaints against violating States to be brought before the eighteen-member Human Rights Committee (**HRC**), a human rights treaty body with the power to: (i) review reports on compliance submitted by States party to the ICCPR and issue its "Observations"; (ii) issue "General Comments" on the implementation of the ICCPR; and (iii) under the (First) Optional Protocol to the ICCPR, the HRC may consider petitions from individuals claiming to be victims of violations of the ICCPR by a State party to the Convention if the individuals have exhausted the available domestic remedies. The HRC may study the matter and then send its views to the petitioner and to the State, but its views are not binding and only hold the weight of the "views" of the Committee.

(iii) International Covenant on Economic, Social and Cultural Rights (ICESCR)

(a) Overview

The ICESCR, which took in 1976, includes a series of economic rights, including the right to work and join trade unions. States party agree to the "progressive realization" of these rights. There is thus an affirmative obligation to *take steps* "to the maximum of its available resources" toward the progressive realization of these rights.

The rights and freedoms guaranteed by the ICESCR include the right to just and favorable conditions of work (Art. 7 ICESCR), to social security (Art. 9 ICESCR), to an adequate standard of living (Art. 11 ICESCR), to enjoyment of the highest standard of physical and mental health (Art. 12 ICESCR) and to free education (Art. 13 ICESCR).

The UN Committee on Economic, Social and Cultural Rights (**CESCR**) monitors implementation of the ICESCR.

(b) States Party

As of April 2011, 160 nations have ratified the ICESCR. Six countries, including Cuba, South Africa and the US, have signed, but not ratified, the ICESCR. States that neither signed nor ratified the ICESCR include Botswana, Haiti, Malaysia, Mayanmar (Burma), Mozambique, Oman, Pakistan, Saudi Arabia, the United Arab Emirates and Western Sahara.

(d) Convention on the Elimination of All Forms of Racial Discrimination (1966)

The International Convention on the Elimination of All Forms of Racial Discrimination (**ICERD**) is a UN convention that was adopted in 1966 and entered into force in 1969. It commits its members to the elimination of racial discrimination and the promotion of understanding among all races.

The Convention includes an individual complaints mechanism, making it enforceable against its parties. The human rights treaty body charged with monitoring and implementing the Convention is the Committee on the Elimination of Racial Discrimination (CERD), which in many ways parallels the mechanisms and procedures of the HRC.

(e) Convention on the Elimination of All Forms of Discrimination Against Women (1979)

The Convention on the Elimination of all Forms of Discrimination against Women (**CEDAW**) is an international convention adopted by the UN General Assembly in 1979 and entering into force in 1981. It is often described as an "international bill of rights for women." It is a nearly universal convention, with only 7 UN member States that have not ratified it: Iran, Nauru, Palau, Somalia, Sudan, Tonga and the United States. The implementation of the Convention is monitored by the Committee on the Elimination of Discrimination Against Women (CEDAW), which parallels the mechanisms and procedures of the HRC.

(f) Convention on the Rights of the Child (1989)

The UN Convention on the Rights of the Child (**UNCRC**) is a human rights treaty setting out the civil, political, economic, social and cultural rights of children, defined as any person under the age of eighteen, unless an earlier age of majority is recognized by a country's law. The

Convention was adopted in 1989 and became effective in 1990. Its two optional protocols were adopted in 2000.

The Convention and its protocols is monitored by the UN Committee on the Rights of the Child (CRC), which is composed of members from countries around the world. Once a year, the Committee submits a report to the UN General Assembly, which also hears a statement from the CRC Chair and the GA adopts a Resolution on the Rights of the Child.

(2) Regional Treaties

(a) Overview

In addition to international treaties providing for the protection of human rights, various instruments apply on a regional basis. These regional instruments include the following:

- European Convention on Human Rights (1950)
- American Convention on Human Rights (1969)
- African Charter on Human and Peoples' Rights (1981)
- Arab Charter on Human Rights (1994)
- Charter of Fundamental Rights of the European Union (2000)

Of these, the Arab Charter on Human Rights provides protections to Palestinian refugees living in Arab States.

(b) Arab Charter on Human Rights (1994)

The Arab Charter on Human Rights was adopted by the Arab League in 1994 and entered into force in 2008. It reaffirms the principles contained in the CUN, the UDHR and the ICCPR. The Preamble also reaffirms the Cairo Declaration on Human Rights in Islam (1990), which specifies human rights in the context of a State governed by *Shari'a*. The Charter recognizes traditional human rights, such as the right to liberty and security of persons, *equality of persons before the law*, protection of persons from torture and the right to property, but Article 27 allows for restrictions on freedom of religion, thought and opinion, when imposed by law.

B. Example of the Application of Human Rights Treaties to Refugees: The Right to Housing

In cases where refugees' rights are not protected in national legislation, such rights are often guaranteed under international law, which could take the form of international treaties that host countries may have ratified, persuasive sources of international law, customary international law or any combination of the three.

One may draw on the example of refugees' rights to adequate housing free from discrimination. Persuasive sources of international law that guarantee this right include the Universal Declaration of Human Rights (**UDHR**), which sets forth a right to "a standard of living adequate for the health and well-being of [each individual] and his family" (Art. 25.1 UDHR). International treaties, including the International Covenant on Economic, Social and Cultural Rights (**ICESCR**), require States party to guarantee the "right of everyone to an adequate standard of living ... including adequate ... housing" (Art. 11.1 ICESCR). The right to "adequate housing" was also reiterated by the Committee on Economic, Social and Cultural Rights with respect to the 1991 Sixth session of the International Covenant on Civil and Political Rights (**ICCPR**) (UN Doc. E/1992/23).

Moreover, the International Convention on the Elimination of All Forms of Racial Discrimination (**ICERD**) requires States party to "prohibit and eliminate racial discrimination in all its forms and to guarantee the right of everyone, without distinction as to race, colour, or national or ethnic origin, to equality before the law, notably in the enjoyment of the ... right to housing" (Art. 5 ICERD).

C. Collective and Individual Rights of Palestinian Refugees under International Law

1. Collective Rights: Self-Determination and State Sovereignty

a) Overview

Military intervention in a foreign State has traditionally been an affront to one of the original general principles of law—state sovereignty. However, there are times when invading a foreign State is justified, such as when such military action is necessary for a State's self-defense or when it is justified as retaliation after an attack. Yet even in such cases, an invasion cannot abolish a vanquished people's right to sovereignty and self-determination.

Thus, although the Zionists conquered 78% of Palestine in the 1948 Arab-Israeli War and occupied the remaining portions of Palestine—the West Bank, East Jerusalem and the Gaza Strip—in the 1967 Six-Day War, Palestinians are entitled under international law to their collective rights of self-determination and state sovereignty on their historic national territory.

b) Legal Basis

(1) Overview

United Nations General Assembly Resolution 181 (II) of 1947 recommended partition of Palestine into a Jewish State and a Palestinian Arab State. It passed by 33 votes for, 13 against, and 10 abstentions. The Palestinian Arabs did not accept the Partition Plan, while the Zionists did.

For Palestinians and other Arabs in the early years following the 1948 Arabic-Israeli War, the focus was on the individual right of return of Palestinian Refugees as was demanded by UN GA Resolution 194 (III) of 11 December 1948. For these Palestinians and other Arabs, return encompassed the restoration of Palestinian national self-determination in historic Palestine. With the establishment of the PLO in 1964, the focus for Palestinians became the liberation of Palestine and the establishment of a State in Palestine.

(2) UN GA Resolution 2787 of 1971 Affirming the Right to Self-Determination

The Palestinian struggle to achieve self-determination in Palestine was given legitimacy by United Nations Resolution 2787 of 6 December 1971, which was reaffirmed in UN GA Resolution 2955 (XXVII) of 12 December 1972. The 1971 resolution:

- Confirmed the legality of the peoples' struggle for self-determination and liberation from colonial and foreign domination and alien subjugation by all available means consistent with the Charter of the United Nations;
- Affirmed man's basic right to fight for the self-determination of his people;
- Called upon all States dedicated to freedom and peace to give all their political, moral and material assistance to peoples struggling for liberation, self-determination and independence.

(3) UN GA Resolution 3236 (XXIX) of 1974 Affirming Self-Determination, Sovereignty and the Right of Return

After the 1973 war, Yasser Arafat and the PLO began to adopt a two-State solution. Arafat addressed the UN GA in 1974, after which the two-State solution was largely supported. Arafat's address was followed by UN GA Resolution 3236 (XXIX) of 22 November 1974, which "reaffirms the inalienable rights of the Palestinian people in Palestine," including the rights to:

- Self-determination without external interference (a collective right);
- National independence and sovereignty (a collective right);
- Return to their homes and property (an individual right).

(4) UN SC Resolution 242 of 1967 Emphasizing the Inadmissibility of the Acquisition of Territory by War

The Palestine National Council (the Parliamentary Body of the Palestine Liberation Organization) voted to declare a Palestinian State rooted in the UN GA Resolution 181 (II) Partition Plan of 1947. A part of the Palestinian declaration was acceptance of UN SC Resolution 242 of 22 November 1967. The PLO thus recognized the State of Israel for the first time, hence solidifying the two-State solution.

UN SC 242 also emphasized the:

- "inadmissibility of the acquisition of territory by war and the need to work for a just and lasting peace in which every State in the area can live in security";
- "withdrawal of Israel armed forces from territories occupied in the recent conflict";
- "necessity for achieving a just settlement of the refugee problem."

2. Individual Rights: The Individual Right of Return

a) *Overview*

Before, during and after the 1948 war, 83% of the indigenous Palestinians (approximately 750,000) became known as the "1948 refugees." These refugees are individually entitled by international refugee laws to realize their right of return—returning to their homes and property and receiving compensation for damage done thereto.

b) *Legal Basis*

Recognizing its special responsibility for the Palestinian refugees, whose plight resulted from the UN GA Resolution 181 (II) Partition Plan and the subsequent 1948 Arab-Israeli War, the UN GA adopted Resolution 194 (III) of 1948, calling for the establishment of the UNCCP, and "Resolving that Jerusalem Should Be Placed Under a Permanent International Regime, and Resolving That the Refugees Should Be Permitted to Return to Their Homes". Resolution 194 (III) further (¶ 11):

> Resolves that the refugees wishing to return to their homes and live at peace with their neighbours should be permitted to do so at the earliest practicable date, and that compensation should be paid for the property of those choosing not to return and for loss of or damage to property which, under principles of international law or in equity, should be made good by the Governments or authorities responsible;
> Instructs the Conciliation Commission to facilitate the repatriation, resettlement and economic and social rehabilitation of the refugees and the payment of compensation, and to maintain close relations with the Director of the United Nations Relief for Palestine Refugees and, through him, with the appropriate organs and agencies of the United Nations.

Recognizing that the Refugees required assistance until such time as Resolution 194 (III), Paragraph 11, would be carried out, the UN GA passed Resolution 302 (IV) in 1949 establishing UNRWA, which was intended to be temporary until the repatriation (or resettlement) of refugees was effected.

Thus, unlike other refugee groups, the Palestinians were singled out for special treatment by providing them with two U.N. agencies, rather than one. The UNCCP was to provide legal protection for the refugees, represent their interests, and implement Resolution 194 (III) with respect to durable solutions. UNRWA was to provide assistance through direct relief and works projects until a durable solution was realized.

UNHCR has refused to provide advocacy to Palestinian Refugees on the basis that the 1950 UNHCR Statute prevents it from doing so with respect to any group of refugees that receives assistance and protection from any other UN agency.[7] Yet the deprivation of UNHCR legal protection in no way negates the absolute legal and inalienable right of each Palestinian refugee to return to his/her home/property in Israel proper and to full compensation under UN GA Resolution 194 (III) and all of the refugee conventions and laws to which it is tied. The issue is representation. The PLO has claimed to represent the interests of all Palestinians. Some feared PLO Chairman Arafat would sign away the Palestinian right of return in return for the collective right to self-determination and state sovereignty.

In any case, under refugee law principles, the interests of refugees should be separately represented in negotiations involving their long-term solutions. The representation issue for the refugees should be resolved as soon as possible, either by UNHCR accepting its protective role or by the creation of a separate body directly authorized by the refugees to carry out their wishes.

---

[7] The 1950 UNHCR Statute states that the competence of the High Commissioner shall not extend to a person who "continues to receive from other organs or agencies of the United Nations protection or assistance" (¶ 7(c) UN GA Resolution 428 (V)).

The CRSR states that that the Convention "shall not apply to persons who are at present receiving from organs or agencies of the United Nations other than the United Nations High Commissioner for Refugees protection or assistance.

"When such protection or assistance has ceased for any reason, without the position of such persons being definitively settled in accordance with the relevant resolutions adopted by the General Assembly of the United Nations, these persons shall *ipso facto* be entitled to the benefits of this Convention" (Art. 1.D CRSR).

D. Conclusions

Nothing in UN SC Resolution 242 legally revokes the Partition Plan under UN GA Resolution 181 (II) or Palestinians' collective rights to sovereignty and self-determination and individual rights of return under UN GA Resolution 194 (III) of 1948, Resolution 2787 of 1971 and Resolution 3236 of 1974. Rather, Resolution 242 merely calls for Israel's withdrawal from the territories occupied in the 1967 Six-Day War.

The PLO may have been willing to concede to Israel the portions of land partitioned to Palestine under Resolution 181 (II) of 1947 and instead accept state sovereignty in the territories occupied by Israel in the 1967 Six-Day War (East Jerusalem, the West Bank and Gaza Strip). Yet the PLO never conceded Palestinians' individual right of return memorialized in UN GA Resolution 194 (III), which aimed to "facilitate the repatriation, resettlement and economic and social rehabilitation of the refugees and the payment of compensation."

Therefore, full recognition of the collective and individual rights of Palestinians under international law would include realizing not only the *collective rights of state sovereignty and self-determination*, but also the *individual right of return*, which should never be viewed as mutually-exclusive rights under international law.

Chapter 5. Challenges Facing UNRWA and Palestinian Refugees

A. Exclusion of Palestinians from the International Refugee Framework

1. Overview

Israel's 1952 Citizenship Law effectively denationalized 1948 Palestinian refugees and their descendants by establishing eligibility criteria for Israeli citizenship that those refugees could not possibly fulfill (*i.e.*, the presence in Israel on the day the law was adopted). Palestinian refugees displaced by the 1948 Arab-Israeli War are unable to realize their right of return absent Israel's recognition of the same. Moreover, Israel continues to occupy and exercise control over the movement of Palestinians within, from and to the oPt, thereby preventing 1967 refugees from returning to these areas.

At the same time, no international agency currently advocates for ending the Palestinian refugee crisis by exploring durable solutions, including the right of Palestinians to repatriation or resettlement, as laid out in UN GA Resolution 194 (III) of 1948.

2. Specialized Regimes for Palestinian Refugees

As a general rule, responsibility for the international protection of refugees is shared between the country of refuge and international organizations, which in most cases is the UN High Commissioner for Refugees (**UNHCR**). In the case of Palestinian refugees, however, the UN General Assembly has created two specialized protection regimes:

a) Durable solutions (protection) framework: UNCCP (1948)

In 1948, the UN Conciliation Commission for Palestine (**UNCCP**) was charged with the "protection of the rights, property and interests of the refugees" displaced in the 1948 Israeli-Arab War, to facilitate durable solutions and continue to carry out the work that was started by UN Mediator Folke Bernadotte prior to his assassination. The UNCCP was thus entrusted with the protection function that for refugees other than Palestinians would normally be assigned to UNHCR.

In Resolution 194 (III) of 1948, which created the UNCCP, the UN GA (¶ 11):

> Resolve[d] that the refugees *wishing to return to their homes* and live at peace with their neighbours should be *permitted to do so* at the earliest practicable date, and that compensation should be paid for the property of those choosing not to return and for loss of or damage to property ...
> Instruct[ed] the Conciliation Commission to facilitate the *repatriation*, *resettlement* and economic and social rehabilitation of the refugees and the payment of compensation ...

The UNCCP was thus created with the mandate to facilitate either the repatriation of Palestinian refugees wishing to return to their homes or the resettlement of those wishing not to return. Every UN Resolution concerning the Palestinians drafted when the UNCCP, UNHCR and UNRWA were created affirms the consensus of the UN that the Palestinian problem would be resolved by one of these durable solutions, with the preference being for the repatriation of Palestinian refugees to their homes, thus fulfilling their right of return.

The UNCCP struggled to fulfill its mandate was however impeded by a stalemate on the part of Arab States and Palestinians, who insisted on full repatriation, and Israel, which refused to accept the repatriation of Palestinians. By 1953, within four years of its formation, the UNCCP practically ceased to function or search for a durable solution to the Palestinian refugee problem.

b)   Aid and protection (assistance) framework: UNRWA (1949)

The UN Relief and Works Agency for Palestinian Refugees in the Near East (**UNRWA**) was created by UN GA Resolution 302 (IV) dated 8 December 1949 and began operations in 1950 with the mandate to provide assistance and protection through relief and jobs to 652,000 Arabs who fled or were expelled from Israel during the Arab-Israeli War.[8]

3. Result: Exclusion of Palestinian Refugees from UNHCR Advocacy and the Refugee Convention

a) Inapplicability of UNHCR Protection

Under UN GA Resolution 428 (V) of 1950, which created UNHCR and set forth its Statute, the competence of UNHCR does not extend to any person who "continues to receive from other organs or agencies of the United Nations protection or assistance" (¶ 7(c) Resolution 428 (V)). Under the prevailing interpretation of this paragraph, the Palestinian refugees are not entitled to UNHCR protection because they have historically received protection from the UNCCP and, while that protection was ineffective and abortive, Palestinian refugees continue to receive assistance from UNRWA.

b) Inapplicability of the Refugee Convention

Under prevailing interpretations of the CRSR, the Convention, like the UNHCR Statute, does not extend or apply to Palestinian refugees. Under Article 1.D of the CRSR, it does not:

> apply to persons who are *at present* receiving from organs or agencies of the United Nations other than the United Nations High Commissioner for Refugees protection or assistance.
> When such protection or assistance has ceased for any reason, without the position of such persons being definitively settled in accordance with the relevant resolutions adopted by the General Assembly of the United Nations, these persons shall ipso facto be entitled to the benefits of this Convention.

Therefore, UNHCR, created in 1950, does not apply to Palestinian refugees and will not apply as long as they continue to receive either protection from the UNCCP or assistance from UNRWA. Since Palestinian refugees continue to receive assistance from UNRWA in the

---

[8] 10 January 2007, "Palestinian Refugee Children: International Protection and Durable Solutions," *Information and Discussion Brief*, No. 10 (Badil Resource Center for Palestinian Residency and Refugee Rights), p. 6.

form of direct relief and works projects, the CRSR does not apply to them.

4. Alternate Interpretation

a) Overview

Not all commentators agree with the conclusion that Palestinian refugees are excluded from UNHCR advocacy and the CRSR. According to an alternate interpretation, the CRSR does at present apply to Palestinian refugees because under Art. 1.D.II CRSR, when the "protection or assistance" provided by organs or agencies of the UN other than UNHCR has "has ceased for any reason, without the position of such persons being definitively settled in accordance with the relevant resolutions adopted by the General Assembly of the United Nations, these persons *shall ipso* facto be entitled to the benefits of this Convention." Under this argument, because the protection afforded to Palestinians under the UNCCP has effectively ceased since the early 1950s, ¶ 2 of Art. 1.D of the CRSR applies, since the mere discontinuation of either "protection *or* assistance" triggers application of the CRSR to the refugee population in question. Therefore, the fact that UNRWA intervenes on their behalf is immaterial because UNRWA only provides "assistance" within the limited meaning of the CRSR—aid in the form of meeting refugees' basic daily needs such as food, clothing and shelter, rather than "protection" in the form of advocacy in the search for durable solutions. Palestinian refugees at present receive no protection from any UN organ or agency and are thus entitled to the protections afforded by the CRSR. This is the interpretation adopted by Professor Susan M. Akram,[9] among others.

---

[9] *See* "Reinterpreting Palestinian Refugee Rights under International Law, and a Framework for Durable Solutions," *BADIL – Information & Discussion Brief,* Issue No. 1, Feb. 2000.

b)   Problems with this Interpretation

There are several problems with the alternate interpretation outlined above. Some of these issues include:

(1) UN GA Resolution 428 (V) 1950

A case can be made that the use of "or" in Art. 1.D of the CRSR ("When such protection or assistance has ceased for any reason, without the position of such persons being definitively settled in accordance with the relevant resolutions adopted by the General Assembly of the United Nations, these persons shall ipso facto be entitled to the benefits of this Convention") implies that given the discontinuation of UNCCP protection for Palestinian refugees, the CRSR now applies to Palestinians, despite continued UNRWA assistance.

However, the conjunction "or" has a very different meaning in UN GA Resolution 428 (V) of 1950, as the condition set forth is a positive condition rather than a negative condition, as is the case of Art. 1.D of the CRSR. Resolution 428 (V) states that the competency of UNHCR shall not extend to a person who "continues to receive from other organs or agencies of the United Nations protection or assistance" (¶ 7 Resolution 428 (V)). In this case, the receipt of *either* protection *or* assistance is a condition that disqualifies a refugee from UNHCR protection.

(2) *De Facto* Expansion of UNRWA's Mandate to Include Basic Protection

While the UNRWA mandate provided in UN GA Resolution 302 (IV) of 1949 has not been amended by subsequent resolutions to include intervention beyond "direct relief and works programmes" (¶ 7 Resolution 302 (IV)), there has been a *de facto* expansion of the mandate by virtue of requests of the international community for UNRWA to take on broader responsibilities. As a result, UNRWA has adopted a flexible reading of the Resolution 302 (IV) mandate, often in response to requests to provide protection by, for example, the UN Secretary General (*see, e.g.*, UN Doc. S/19443, 10). Such interventions in the area of protection date back as early as the 1950s, when UNRWA facilitated some small-scale resettlements through a Placement Services Office that offered loans and other assistance to Palestinian refugees seeking to resettle in Iraq or Libya (*see* UN Doc. A/2171) (*see* "Expanded Reading of Resolution 302 (IV) to Include Basic Protection," *infra.*, for full discussion).

Therefore, because UNRWA has over the past decades been providing Palestinian refugees with protection, albeit basic and limited protection, neither the UNHCR Statute nor the CRSR apply to Palestinian refugees because they continue to receive assistance and protection from a UN agency other than UNHCR.

5. Observations and Consequence: Humanitarian Action without a Durable Solution

While this interpretation is based on a reasoned reading of the texts, it is not the prevailing interpretation, which holds that UNHCR is not authorized to act on behalf of Palestinian refugees because protection is being provided, at least in theory, by the UNCCP and, in any case, UNRWA is providing assistance to Palestinian refugees.

The result of this interpretation is that there is a shortfall of protection in the form of durable solutions to the Palestinian refugee crisis. The protection measures that are offered often take the form of political negotiations brokered by global powers, which themselves often become politicized.

The result has been humanitarian action on the part of UNRWA without a solution to the forced displacement of Palestinian refugees. Such action, without a political resolution, cannot on its own come to solve the Palestinian refugee problem.

B. Funding: Voluntary Contributions

Since UNRWA is funded almost entirely by voluntary contributions rather than by mandatory assessments, UNRWA must actively seek funding from donors. Yet UNRWA has been consistently underfunded during the past decade, which has had a negative impact on UNRWA's ability to deliver the quality of required services. This has had an impact on the healthcare, social well-being and education of refugees. For example, a program providing scholarships for university studies in Middle East countries has been discontinued. More than three quarters of UNRWA schools operate on a double shift basis due to a shortage of school buildings. Moreover, the working conditions and resources available are inferior to those in schools run by the host countries, thus making it more difficult to recruit teachers.

UNRWA is thus eagerly seeking additional funding. The UNRWA private partnership unit (Partnerships Division) works to support the organization from a financial perspective.

C. Caseload

1. Additional Burden Due to the Syrian Civil War

In addition to the overburdened caseload that UNRWA is handling, the Syrian conflict presents a new set of challenges in working with Palestinian refugees in Syria: access, security of persons, basic necessities of life and the outflow of refugees from Syria into Lebanon, where 1 million refugees have entered a population of 4.5 million with a current caseload of 250,000 Palestinian refugees) and Jordan.

2. Numerous Healthcare and Other Needs of Refugees

A major challenge facing UNRWA is the high number of refugees visiting health centers, vocational and training centers, rehabilitation centers, women's program centers and other programs. There are high numbers of daily patients' visits to health centers, which leads to a heavy workload of doctors and other healthcare staff. The average number of consultations to UNRWA health and dental centers exceeds 1.5 million per year.

D. Military Occupation and Gaza Blockade

The continued military occupation of the West Bank and Gaza Strip along with the Gaza Blockade further complicate the work of UNRWA on many levels. The military occupation impedes UNRWA from providing educational experiences within a physical and psycho-social environment that is safe and secure. Israeli restrictions of movement or military incursions have added pressure to UNRWA's schools and lead to significant lost teacher days. For example, between 1 July 2004 and 30 June 2005, UNRWA's 93 schools in the West Bank reported 1,939 lost teacher days and Gaza's 180 schools experienced 27,508 lost teacher days (*Report of the Commissioner-General of the United Nations Relief and Works Agency for Palestine Refugees in the Near East*, June 2005, paras. 235-36). The Wall and other restrictions of movement impede the ability of refugees in West Bank and Gaza Strip to access health services, since UNRWA is unable to access thousands of Palestinians in the area between the Green Line and the Wall. Furthermore, the Gaza Blockage restricts UNRWA's ability to import materials needed to maintain and improve camp infrastructure and repair buildings damaged as a result of conflict. Lack of access to services and restrictions of movement often results in refugees' further displacement as they voluntarily leave their homes.

E. Other Challenges

Other challenges to UNRWA's work include forcible resettlement, house demolition and the Wall in the West Bank, which further restrict movement of Palestinians, create new waives of internally displaced persons and increase tensions between Palestinians and Jews.

F. Result: Shortfall of Assistance and Protection

As a result of the multiple challenges facing UNRWA and Palestinian refugees, Palestinian refugees suffer from severe shortfalls in assistance and protection. UNRWA faces constant challenges fulfilling basic needs in meeting its assistance mandate. With respect to protection, the UNCCP continues to apply in theory, but practically, it has ceased to function, protect or search for durable solutions. UNHCR, which excludes from its mandate all Palestinian refugees living in camps administered by UNRWA or any other UN organs or agencies, does not assist the UNCCP in its search for durable solutions. As a result, Palestinian refugees currently face both shortfalls in assistance and are left in a framework where no global body actively advocates for a solution to their plight.

Appendices

Glossary

Al-Aqsa Intifada *See* SECOND INTIFADA.

Balfour Declaration 1917 declaration by British Foreign Minister Lord Balfour that stated that the British government viewed "with favour the establishment in Palestine of a national home for the Jewish people."

British Mandate of Palestine Legal instrument that formalized and recognized British rule over the geopolitical entity known as MANDATE PALESTINE. The Council of the League of Nations issued its consent to MANDATE PALESTINE on 24 July 1922, followed by the 16 September 1922 Transjordan Memorandum. The BRITISH MANDATE OF PALESTINE came into effect in 1923, following the ratification of the Treaty of Lausanne. The mandate continued until the 1948 creation of Israel. *Compare* MANDATE PALESTINE.

Deir Yassin massacre Massacre during the civil war that preceded the end of MANDATE PALESTINE that took place on 9 April 1948 when militants from Zionist paramilitary groups attacked Deir Yassin, an Arab village of approximately several hundred people just west of Jerusalem. The event was seen as triggering the intervention of Arab countries in the civil war, thus transforming the civil conflict into the Arab-Israeli War of 1948.

Durable solutions Any of the three solutions that end the problems associated with displacement for the refugee and allow her to resume a normal life in a safe environment. There are three traditional durable solutions available for consideration: voluntary repatriation, local integration and resettlement.

First Intifada Palestinian uprising against the Israeli occupation of the oPt lasting from 1987 until the Madrid Conference of 1991, or, alternatively, the signing of the Oslo Accords in 1993 though some date its conclusion to 1993, with the signing of the Oslo Accords. The First Intifada began when tensions in Jabalia Refugee Camp in northern Gaza reached a boiling point when an IDF truck struck a civilian car resulting in the death of four Palestinians. In response, Palestinians boycotted Israeli civil institutions, refused to work in Israeli settlements or to pay taxes, and engaged in graffiti and the throwing of stones and Molotov cocktails at the IDF and its infrastructure within the Palestinian territories. Israel responded by deploying some 80,000 soldier to quash the rebellion. *See* SECOND INTIFADA.

Gaza War May refer to any of the following conflicts between Israel and the Hamas-controlled Palestinian territory in the Gaza Strip: (i) 2008–09 conflict lasting 22 days, also known as OPERATION CAST LEAD; (ii) 2012 conflict, also known as Operation Pillar of Defense; (iii) 2014 Israel–Gaza conflict, also known as Operation Protective Edge.

Inter-Agency Standing Committee (IASC) Inter-agency forum of UN and non-UN humanitarian partners founded in 1992 by the UN GA to strengthen humanitarian assistance and improve the delivery of humanitarian assistance to affected populations.

Mandate Palestine Geopolitical entity under British administration, carved out of Ottoman Southern Syria after World War I and continued from 1920 until the 1948 creation of Israel. *Also known as* Mandatory Palestine and British Palestine. *Compare* BRITISH MANDATE OF PALESTINE.

Non-refoulement Principle that establishes a refugee's non-derogable right to be protected against forcible return to territories where his or her life or freedom would be in danger. This principle places an absolute obligation on States party to the CRSR not to return refugees to countries in which such danger to their lives or freedom would arise.

Operation Cast Lead 22-day Israeli military assault on the Gaza Strip that began on Dec. 27, 2008, and went into January 2009, in which Israel used white phosphorus in heavily-populated civilian areas. In the aftermath of the offensive, a UN-appointed fact finding mission found strong evidence of war crimes and crimes against humanity committed by both the Israeli military and Palestinian militias.

Oslo Accords Set of agreements that were secretly negotiated between the PLO and Israel in 1993. Their signature was followed by a public ceremony in Washington D.C. on 13 September 1993 with Yasser Arafat and Yitzhak Rabin. The Accords granted the Palestinians a right to self-government on the Gaza Strip and in Jericho in the West Bank through the creation of the PALESTINIAN AUTHORITY.

Palestinian Authority (PA) Administrative body providing for the self-government of Palestinians in the Gaza Strip and Jericho in the West Bank and created by the 1993 Oslo Accords that were secretly negotiated between the PLO and Israel. *Compare* PALESTINE LIBERATION ORGANIZATION.

Palestine Liberation Organization (PLO) Organization founded in 1964 with the purpose of liberating Palestine. It is recognized as the sole legitimate representative of the Palestinians by over 100 states, with which it holds diplomatic relations, and has enjoyed observer status at the United Nations since 1974. The headquarters of the PLO were moved to Ramallah on the West Bank. Compare PALESTINIAN AUTHORITY.

Palestine National Council Parliamentary Body of the PALESTINE LIBERATION ORGANIZATION (PLO).

Sabra and Shatila massacre Widespread massacre that took place from 16 to 18 September 1982 by a militia affiliated with the a predominantly Christian Lebanese right-wing Kataeb Party in the Sabra neighborhood and Shatila Refugee Camp in Beirut, resulting in the deaths of between 762 and 3,500 mostly Palestinian and Shi'ite civilians.

Second Intifada Second Palestinian uprising against Israeli occupation, which began in September 2000, when Ariel Sharon made a visit to the Temple Mount, seen by Palestinians as highly provocative. Palestinian demonstrators subsequently threw stones at police and were dispersed by the Israeli army using tear gas and rubber bullets. Intensified fighting between Israeli and Palestinians continued through 2005. Also known as AL-AQSA INTIFADA. See FIRST INTIFADA.

United Nations Administrative Tribunal (UNAT) Court established by the UN GA as the final arbiter over claims alleging breach of the terms of appointment (including all pertinent regulations and rules) of staff members working in the UN Secretariat. 30 June 2009 marked the end of the mandate of the United Nations Administrative Tribunal, which was replaced by the UNITED NATIONS APPEALS TRIBUNAL (UNAT) from 1 July 2009 onwards.

United Nations Appeals Tribunal (UNAT) Court of second instance within the UN internal justice system, hearing cases in which a court of first instance allegedly exceeded its jurisdiction, failed to exercise its jurisdiction or erred on questions of fact, procedure or law. It became operational on 1 July 2009, replacing the UNITED NATIONS ADMINISTRATIVE TRIBUNAL. See UNITED NATIONS DISPUTE TRIBUNAL (UNDT).

United Nations Conciliation Commission for Palestine UN commission established by RESOLUTION 194 (III) OF 1948 and charged with the "protection of the rights, property and interests of the refugees" displaced in the 1948 Israeli-Arab War and to facilitate durable solutions.

United Nations Dispute Tribunal (UNDT) Court of first instance within the UN internal justice system that became operational on 1 July 2009 with the power to hear cases appealing administrative decisions alleged to be non-compliant with terms of appointment or employment contracts filed by staff members of the UN Secretariat; Peacekeeping and Political Missions; International Criminal Tribunals; ECOSOC Regional Commissions; and GA Programs, Organs, Funds and Other Entities. The Tribunal conducts hearings, issues orders, and renders binding judgments. Staff members and the UN Administration may appeal the judgments of the United Nations Dispute Tribunal to the UNITED NATIONS APPEALS TRIBUNAL. *Compare* UNRWA DISPUTE TRIBUNAL.

United Nations Partition Plan for Palestine Proposal developed by the UN that recommended a partition with economic union of Mandate Palestine to follow the termination of the BRITISH MANDATE OF PALESTINE. On 29 November 1947, the UN GA adopted RESOLUTION 181 (II), recommending the adoption and implementation of the PARTITION PLAN FOR PALESTINE with the votes of 33 nations in favor, 13 opposed and 10 abstentions.

United Nations Relief and Works Agency for Palestine Refugees in the Near East (UNRWA) Agency established by the General Assembly in 1949 to provide assistance and protection through relief and jobs to 652,000 Arabs who fled or were expelled from Israel during the Arab-Israeli War. Today, UNRWA provides assistance to some five million Palestinian refugees living in the West Bank, the Gaza Strip, Jordan, Lebanon and Syria to achieve their full potential in human development, pending a just and durable solution to their plight.

UNRWA Dispute Tribunal Court of first instance that hears and decides cases filed by or on behalf of UNRWA staff members appealing administrative decisions alleged to be non-compliant with their terms of appointment or employment contracts. Staff members and the UNRWA Administration may appeal the judgments of the UNRWA Dispute Tribunal to the UNITED NATIONS APPEALS TRIBUNAL. *Compare* UNITED NATIONS DISPUTE TRIBUNAL.

Charts and Graphs

Palestinian Refugees in Facts and Figures

Largest group of refugees worldwide	Palestinian
Percentage of worldwide refugees that are Palestinian	One in three
Number of Palestinian refugees worldwide	6.5 million
Number of Syrian refugees worldwide	2.6 million[10]
Number of Palestinian refugees that received assistance from UNRWA	~ 5 million
Number of Palestinian refugees and their descendants displaced in 1948 that are registered for humanitarian assistance with the UN	Over 3.8 million
Number of Palestinian refugees and their descendants, also displaced in 1948, that are not registered with the UN	1.5 million
Number of Palestinians and their descendants that are internally displaced within Israel	263,000

Timelines

Palestinian/Arab-Israeli Wars

Arab-Israeli Wars

1948–1949	First Arab–Israeli War
1956	Suez War
1967	The Six-Day War
1973	Yom Kippur War

Israeli-Palestinian Armed Conflicts

1987–1993	First Intifada
2000–2005	Second Intifada (Al-Aqsa Intifada)

---

[10] This figure, which is constantly increasing, is current as of the time of this writing.

2008–2009	First Gaza War (Operation Cast Lead)
2012	Second Gaza War (Operation Pillar of Defense)
2014	Third Gaza War (Operation Protective Edge)

Palestinian Refugee Framework Milestones

Phase I: World War I and the establishment of Mandate Palestine

1914	Beginning of World War I
1918	End of World War I
1920	Establishment of Mandate Palestine (geographical entity) under British administration
1922	British Mandate of Palestine (legal instrument) confirmed by the League of Nations
1923	British Mandate of Palestine comes into effect

Phase II: World War II, the UN Partition Plan and the founding of Israel

1939	Beginning of World War II
1945	Conclusion of World War II; creation of the UN
1947	UN GA Resolution 181(II), recommending the implementation of the Partition Plan for Palestine.
1948	End of Mandate Palestine Israel founded

Phase III: The Arab-Israeli War and the founding of UNCCP and UNRWA

1948	Arab-Israeli War UNCCP founded under UN GA Resolution 194 (III) of 1948
1949	Israel admitted to the UN on 11 May 1949 UNRWA founded and mandated under UN GA Resolution 302 (V) of 8 December 1949
1950	UNRWA began operations

Phase IV: The founding of UNHCR and the Refugee Convention and Protocol

1950	UNHCR founded
1951	Convention Relating to the Status of Refugees (Refugee Convention)
1967	Protocol to the Refugee Convention (Refugee Protocol)

Relevant International Legal Instruments

GA Resolution 181 (II) of 1947	Resolution partitioning Mandate Palestine following the termination of the British Mandate of Palestine. *See* UNITED NATIONS PARTITION PLAN FOR PALESTINE.
GA Resolution 194 (III) of 1948	Resolution calling for the establishment of the UNCCP and instructing the UNCCP to "facilitate the repatriation, resettlement and economic and social rehabilitation of the refugees and the payment of compensation."
GA Resolution 302 (IV) of 1949	Resolution establishing and mandating UNRWA.
GA Resolution 428 (V) of 1950	Resolution adopting the Statute of the United Nations High Commissioner for Refugees
Refugee Convention of 1951	Convention Relating to the Status of Refugees
Refugee Protocol of 1967	Protocol to the Refugee Convention
SC Resolution 242 of 1967	Resolution emphasizing the "inadmissibility of the acquisition of territory by war and the need to work for a just and lasting peace in which every State in the area can live in security" and calling for Israel's withdrawal from the territories occupied in the 1967 Six-Day War.

United Nations Internal Justice System

	Tribunal	Jurisdiction	Notes
Cour ts of	United Nations Dispute	Claims by staff members of the UN Secretariat;	Court of first instance within the UN internal justice system that became operational on 1

	Tribunal (**UNDT**)	Peacekeeping and Political Missions; International Criminal Tribunals; ECOSOC Regional Commissions; and GA Programs, Organs, Funds and Other Entities	July 2009 with the power to hear cases appealing administrative decisions alleged to be non-compliant with terms of appointment or employment contracts.
	UNRWA Dispute Tribunal	Claims filed by UNRWA staff members	Court of first instance that hears and decides cases filed by or on behalf of UNRWA staff members appealing administrative decisions alleged to be non-compliant with their terms of appointment or employment contracts.
Appeals Court	United Nations Appeals Tribunal (**UNAT**)	Appeals to judgments issued by the United Nations Dispute Tribunal and other courts of first instance, such as the UNRWA Dispute Tribunal	Court of second instance within the UN internal justice system, hearing cases in which a court of first instance allegedly exceeded its jurisdiction, failed to exercise its jurisdiction or erred on questions of fact, procedure or law. It became operational on 1 July 2009, replacing the United Nations Administrative Tribunal.

UN General Assembly Resolution 181 (II)

General Assembly
A/RES/181(II)
29 November 1947

Resolution 181 (II). Future government of Palestine

A

The General Assembly,

Having met in special session at the request of the mandatory Power to constitute and instruct a special committee to prepare for the consideration of the question of the future government of Palestine at the second regular session;

Having constituted a Special Committee and instructed it to investigate all questions and issues relevant to the problem of Palestine, and to prepare proposals for the solution of the problem, and

Having received and examined the report of the Special Committee (document A/364) 1/ including a number of unanimous recommendations and a plan of partition with economic union approved by the majority of the Special Committee,

Considers that the present situation in Palestine is one which is likely to impair the general welfare and friendly relations among nations;

Takes note of the declaration by the mandatory Power that it plans to complete its evacuation of Palestine by 1 August 1948;

Recommends to the United Kingdom, as the mandatory Power for Palestine, and to all other Members of the United Nations the adoption and implementation, with regard to the future government of Palestine, of the Plan of Partition with Economic Union set out below;

Requests that

(a) The Security Council take the necessary measures as provided for in the plan for its implementation;

(b) The Security Council consider, if circumstances during the transitional period require such consideration, whether the situation in

Palestine constitutes a threat to the peace. If it decides that such a threat exists, and in order to maintain international peace and security, the Security Council should supplement the authorization of the General Assembly by taking measures, under Articles 39 and 41 of the Charter, to empower the United Nations Commission, as provided in this resolution, to exercise in Palestine the functions which are assigned to it by this resolution;

(c) The Security Council determine as a threat to the peace, breach of the peace or act of aggression, in accordance with Article 39 of the Charter, any attempt to alter by force the settlement envisaged by this resolution;

(d) The Trusteeship Council be informed of the responsibilities envisaged for it in this plan;

Calls upon the inhabitants of Palestine to take such steps as may be necessary on their part to put this plan into effect;

Appeals to all Governments and all peoples to refrain from taking action which might hamper or delay the carrying out of these recommendations, and

Authorizes the Secretary-General to reimburse travel and subsistence expenses of the members of the Commission referred to in Part I, Section B, paragraph 1 below, on such basis and in such form as he may determine most appropriate in the circumstances, and to provide the Commission with the necessary staff to assist in carrying out the functions assigned to the Commission by the General Assembly.

B

The General Assembly

Authorizes the Secretary-General to draw from the Working Capital Fund a sum not to exceed $2,000,000 for the purposes set forth in the last paragraph of the resolution on the future government of Palestine.
Hundred and twenty-eighth plenary meeting
29 November 1947

[At its hundred and twenty-eighth plenary meeting on 29 November 1947 the General Assembly, in accordance with the terms of the above resolution [181 A], elected the following members of the United Nations Commission on Palestine: Bolivia, Czechoslovakia, Denmark, Panama and Philippines.]

PLAN OF PARTITION WITH ECONOMIC UNION

PART I. Future constitution and government of Palestine

A. TERMINATION OF MANDATE, PARTITION AND INDEPENDENCE

1. The Mandate for Palestine shall terminate as soon as possible but in any case not later than 1 August 1948.

2. The armed forces of the mandatory Power shall be progressively withdrawn from Palestine, the withdrawal to be completed as soon as possible but in any case not later than 1 August 1948.

The mandatory Power shall advise the Commission, as far in advance as possible, of its intention to terminate the Mandate and to evacuate each area.

The mandatory Power shall use its best endeavours to ensure than an area situated in the territory of the Jewish State, including a seaport and hinterland adequate to provide facilities for a substantial immigration, shall be evacuated at the earliest possible date and in any event not later than 1 February 1948.

3. Independent Arab and Jewish States and the Special International Regime for the City of Jerusalem, set forth in part III of this plan, shall come into existence in Palestine two months after the evacuation of the armed forces of the mandatory Power has been completed but in any case not later than 1 October 1948. The boundaries of the Arab State, the Jewish State, and the City of Jerusalem shall be as described in parts II and III below.

4. The period between the adoption by the General Assembly of its recommendation on the question of Palestine and the establishment of the independence of the Arab and Jewish States shall be a transitional period.

B. STEPS PREPARATORY TO INDEPENDENCE

1. A Commission shall be set up consisting of one representative of each of five Member States. The Members represented on the Commission shall be elected by the General Assembly on as broad a basis, geographically and otherwise, as possible.

2. The administration of Palestine shall, as the mandatory Power withdraws its armed forces, be progressively turned over to the Commission; which shall act in conformity with the recommendations of the General Assembly, under the guidance of the Security Council. The mandatory Power shall to the fullest possible extent co-ordinate its plans for withdrawal with the plans of the Commission to take over and administer areas which have been evacuated.

In the discharge of this administrative responsibility the Commission shall have authority to issue necessary regulations and take other measures as required.

The mandatory Power shall not take any action to prevent, obstruct or delay the implementation by the Commission of the measures recommended by the General Assembly.

3. On its arrival in Palestine the Commission shall proceed to carry out measures for the establishment of the frontiers of the Arab and Jewish States and the City of Jerusalem in accordance with the general lines of the recommendations of the General Assembly on the partition of Palestine. Nevertheless, the boundaries as described in part II of this plan are to be modified in such a way that village areas as a rule will not be divided by state boundaries unless pressing reasons make that necessary.

4. The Commission, after consultation with the democratic parties and other public organizations of The Arab and Jewish States, shall select and establish in each State as rapidly as possible a Provisional Council of Government. The activities of both the Arab and Jewish Provisional Councils of Government shall be carried out under the general direction of the Commission.

If by 1 April 1948 a Provisional Council of Government cannot be selected for either of the States, or, if selected, cannot carry out its functions, the Commission shall communicate that fact to the Security Council for such action with respect to that State as the Security Council may deem proper, and to the Secretary-General for communication to the Members of the United Nations.

5. Subject to the provisions of these recommendations, during the transitional period the Provisional Councils of Government, acting under the Commission, shall have full authority in the areas under their control, including authority over matters of immigration and land regulation.

6. The Provisional Council of Government of each State acting under the Commission, shall progressively receive from the Commission full responsibility for the administration of that State in the period between the termination of the Mandate and the establishment of the State's independence.

7. The Commission shall instruct the Provisional Councils of Government of both the Arab and Jewish States, after their formation, to proceed to the establishment of administrative organs of government, central and local.

8. The Provisional Council of Government of each State shall, within the shortest time possible, recruit an armed militia from the residents of that State, sufficient in number to maintain internal order and to prevent frontier clashes.

This armed militia in each State shall, for operational purposes, be under the command of Jewish or Arab officers resident in that State, but general political and military control, including the choice of the militia's High Command, shall be exercised by the Commission.

9. The Provisional Council of Government of each State shall, not later than two months after the withdrawal of the armed forces of the mandatory Power, hold elections to the Constituent Assembly which shall be conducted on democratic lines.

The election regulations in each State shall be drawn up by the Provisional Council of Government and approved by the Commission. Qualified voters for each State for this election shall be persons over eighteen years of age who are: (a) Palestinian citizens residing in that State and (b) Arabs and Jews residing in the State, although not Palestinian citizens, who, before voting, have signed a notice of intention to become citizens of such State.

Arabs and Jews residing in the City of Jerusalem who have signed a notice of intention to become citizens, the Arabs of the Arab State and the Jews of the Jewish State, shall be entitled to vote in the Arab and Jewish States respectively.

Women may vote and be elected to the Constituent Assemblies.

During the transitional period no Jew shall be permitted to establish residence in the area of the proposed Arab State, and no Arab shall be permitted to establish residence in the area of the proposed Jewish State, except by special leave of the Commission.

10. The Constituent Assembly of each State shall draft a democratic constitution for its State and choose a provisional government to succeed the Provisional Council of Government appointed by the Commission. The constitutions of the States shall embody chapters 1 and 2 of the Declaration provided for in section C below and include inter alia provisions for:

(a) Establishing in each State a legislative body elected by universal suffrage and by secret ballot on the basis of proportional representation, and an executive body responsible to the legislature;

(b) Settling all international disputes in which the State may be involved by peaceful means in such a manner that international peace and security, and justice, are not endangered;

(c) Accepting the obligation of the State to refrain in its international relations from the threat or use of force against the territorial integrity of political independence of any State, or in any other manner inconsistent with the purposes of the United Nations;

(d) Guaranteeing to all persons equal and non-discriminatory rights in civil, political, economic and religious matters and the enjoyment of human rights and fundamental freedoms, including freedom of religion, language, speech and publication, education, assembly and association;

(e) Preserving freedom of transit and visit for all residents and citizens of the other State in Palestine and the City of Jerusalem, subject to considerations of national security, provided that each State shall control residence within its borders.

11. The Commission shall appoint a preparatory economic commission of three members to make whatever arrangements are possible for economic co-operation, with a view to establishing, as soon as practicable, the Economic Union and the Joint Economic Board, as provided in section D below.

12. During the period between the adoption of the recommendations on the question of Palestine by the General Assembly and the termination of the Mandate, the mandatory Power in Palestine shall maintain full responsibility for administration in areas from which it has not withdrawn its armed forces. The Commission shall assist the mandatory Power in the carrying out of these functions. Similarly the mandatory Power shall co-operate with the Commission in the execution of its functions.

13. With a view to ensuring that there shall be continuity in the functioning of administrative services and that, on the withdrawal of the armed forces of the mandatory Power, the whole administration shall be in the charge of the Provisional Councils and the Joint Economic Board, respectively, acting under the Commission, there shall be a progressive transfer, from the mandatory Power to the Commission, of responsibility for all the functions of government, including that of maintaining law and order in the areas from which the forces of the mandatory Power have been withdrawn.

14. The Commission shall be guided in its activities by the recommendations of the General Assembly and by such instructions as the Security Council may consider necessary to issue.

The measures taken by the Commission, within the recommendations of the General Assembly, shall become immediately effective unless the Commission has previously received contrary instructions from the Security Council.

The Commission shall render periodic monthly progress reports, or more frequently if desirable, to the Security Council.

15. The Commission shall make its final report to the next regular session of the General Assembly and to the Security Council simultaneously.

C. DECLARATION

A declaration shall be made to the United Nations by the provisional government of each proposed State before independence. It shall contain inter alia the following clauses:
General Provision

The stipulations contained in the declaration are recognized as fundamental laws of the State and no law, regulation or official action shall conflict or interfere with these stipulations, nor shall any law, regulation or official action prevail over them.

Chapter 1. Holy Places, religious buildings and sites

1. Existing rights in respect of Holy Places and religious buildings or sites shall not be denied or impaired.

2. In so far as Holy Places are concerned, the liberty of access, visit and transit shall be guaranteed, in conformity with existing rights, to all residents and citizens of the other State and of the City of Jerusalem, as well as to aliens, without distinction as to nationality, subject to requirements of national security, public order and decorum.

Similarly, freedom of worship shall be guaranteed in conformity with existing rights, subject to the maintenance of public order and decorum.

3. Holy Places and religious buildings or sites shall be preserved. No act shall be permitted which may in any way impair their sacred character. If at any time it appears to the Government that any particular Holy Place, religious building or site is in need of urgent repair, the Government may call upon the community or communities concerned to carry out such repair. The Government may carry it out itself at the expense of the community or communities concerned if no action is taken within a reasonable time.

4. No taxation shall be levied in respect of any Holy Place, religious building or site which was exempt from taxation on the date of the creation of the State.

No change in the incidence of such taxation shall be made which would either discriminate between the owners or occupiers of Holy Places, religious buildings or sites, or would place such owners or occupiers in a position less favourable in relation to the general incidence of taxation than existed at the time of the adoption of the Assembly's recommendations.

5. The Governor of the City of Jerusalem shall have the right to determine whether the provisions of the Constitution of the State in relation to Holy Places, religious buildings and sites within the borders of the State and the religious rights appertaining thereto, are being properly applied and respected, and to make decisions on the basis of existing rights in cases of disputes which may arise between the different religious communities or the rites of a religious community with respect to such places, buildings and sites. He shall receive full co-operation and such privileges and immunities as are necessary for the exercise of his functions in the State.

Chapter 2. Religious and Minority Rights

1. Freedom of conscience and the free exercise of all forms of worship, subject only to the maintenance of public order and morals, shall be ensured to all.

2. No discrimination of any kind shall be made between the inhabitants on the ground of race, religion, language or sex.

3. All persons within the jurisdiction of the State shall be entitled to equal protection of the laws.

4. The family law and personal status of the various minorities and their religious interests, including endowments, shall be respected.

5. Except as may be required for the maintenance of public order and good government, no measure shall be taken to obstruct or interfere with the enterprise of religious or charitable bodies of all faiths or to discriminate against any representative or member of these bodies on the ground of his religion or nationality.

6. The State shall ensure adequate primary and secondary education for the Arab and Jewish minority, respectively, in its own language and its cultural traditions.

The right of each community to maintain its own schools for the education of its own members in its own language, while conforming to such educational requirements of a general nature as the State may impose, shall not be denied or impaired. Foreign educational establishments shall continue their activity on the basis of their existing rights.

7. No restriction shall be imposed on the free use by any citizen of the State of any language in private intercourse, in commerce, in religion, in the Press or in publications of any kind, or at public meetings.3/

8. No expropriation of land owned by an Arab in the Jewish State (by a Jew in the Arab State)4/ shall be allowed except for public purposes. In all cases of expropriation full compensation as fixed by the Supreme Court shall be paid previous to dispossession.

Chapter 3. Citizenship, international conventions and financial obligations

1. Citizenship. Palestinian citizens residing in Palestine outside the City of Jerusalem, as well as Arabs and Jews who, not holding Palestinian citizenship, reside in Palestine outside the City of Jerusalem shall, upon the recognition of independence, become citizens of the State in which they are resident and enjoy full civil and political rights. Persons over the age of eighteen years may opt, within one year from the date of recognition of independence of the State in which they reside, for citizenship of the other State, providing that no Arab residing in the area of the proposed Arab State shall have the right to opt for citizenship in the proposed Jewish State and no Jew residing in the proposed Jewish State shall have the right to opt for citizenship in the proposed Arab State. The exercise of this right of option will be taken to include the wives and children under eighteen years of age of persons so opting.

Arabs residing in the area of the proposed Jewish State and Jews residing in the area of the proposed Arab State who have signed a notice of intention to opt for citizenship of the other State shall be eligible to vote in the elections to the Constituent Assembly of that State, but not in the elections to the Constituent Assembly of the State in which they reside.

2. International conventions. (a) The State shall be bound by all the international agreements and conventions, both general and special, to which Palestine has become a party. Subject to any right of denunciation provided for therein, such agreements and conventions shall be respected by the State throughout the period for which they were concluded.

(b) Any dispute about the applicability and continued validity of international conventions or treaties signed or adhered to by the mandatory Power on behalf of Palestine shall be referred to the International Court of Justice in accordance with the provisions of the Statute of the Court.

3. Financial obligations. (a) The State shall respect and fulfil all financial obligations of whatever nature assumed on behalf of Palestine by the mandatory Power during the exercise of the Mandate and recognized by the State. This provision includes the right of public servants to pensions, compensation or gratuities.

(b) These obligations shall be fulfilled through participation in the Joint economic Board in respect of those obligations applicable to Palestine as a whole, and individually in respect of those applicable to, and fairly apportionable between, the States.

(c) A Court of Claims, affiliated with the Joint Economic Board, and composed of one member appointed by the United Nations, one representative of the United Kingdom and one representative of the State concerned, should be established. Any dispute between the United Kingdom and the State respecting claims not recognized by the latter should be referred to that Court.

(d) Commercial concessions granted in respect of any part of Palestine prior to the adoption of the resolution by the General Assembly shall continue to be valid according to their terms, unless modified by agreement between the concession-holder and the State.

Chapter 4. Miscellaneous provisions

1. The provisions of chapters 1 and 2 of the declaration shall be under the guarantee of the United Nations, and no modifications shall be made in them without the assent of the General Assembly of the United nations. Any Member of the United Nations shall have the right to bring to the attention of the General Assembly any infraction or danger of infraction of any of these stipulations, and the General Assembly may thereupon make such recommendations as it may deem proper in the circumstances.

2. Any dispute relating to the application or the interpretation of this declaration shall be referred, at the request of either party, to the International Court of Justice, unless the parties agree to another mode of settlement.

D. ECONOMIC UNION AND TRANSIT

1. The Provisional Council of Government of each State shall enter into an undertaking with respect to economic union and transit. This undertaking shall be drafted by the commission provided for in section B, paragraph 1, utilizing to the greatest possible extent the advice and co-operation of representative organizations and bodies from each of the proposed States. It shall contain provisions to establish the Economic Union of Palestine and provide for other matters of common interest. If by 1 April 1948 the Provisional Councils of Government have not entered into the undertaking, the undertaking shall be put into force by the Commission.

The Economic Union of Palestine

2. The objectives of the Economic Union of Palestine shall be:

(a) A customs union;

(b) A joint currency system providing for a single foreign exchange rate;

(c) Operation in the common interest on a non-discriminatory basis of railways; inter-State highways; postal, telephone and telegraphic services, and port and airports involved in international trade and commerce;

(d) Joint economic development, especially in respect of irrigation, land reclamation and soil conservation;

(e) Access for both States and for the City of Jerusalem on a non-discriminatory basis to water and power facilities.

3. There shall be established a Joint Economic Board, which shall consist of three representatives of each of the two States and three foreign members appointed by the Economic and Social Council of the United Nations. The foreign members shall be appointed in the first instance for a term of three years; they shall serve as individuals and not as representatives of States.

4. The functions of the Joint Economic Board shall be to implement either directly or by delegation the measures necessary to realize the objectives of the Economic Union. It shall have all powers of organization and administration necessary to fulfil its functions.

5. The States shall bind themselves to put into effect the decisions of the Joint Economic Board. The Board's decisions shall be taken by a majority vote.

6. In the event of failure of a State to take the necessary action the Board may, by a vote of six members, decide to withhold an appropriate portion of that part of the customs revenue to which the State in question is entitled under the Economic Union. Should the State persist in its failure to co-operate, the Board may decide by a simple majority vote upon such further sanctions, including disposition of funds which it has withheld, as it may deem appropriate.

7. In relation to economic development, the functions of the Board shall be the planning, investigation and encouragement of joint development projects, but it shall not undertake such projects except with the assent of both States and the City of Jerusalem, in the event that Jerusalem is directly involved in the development project.

8. In regard to the joint currency system the currencies circulating in the two States and the City of Jerusalem shall be issued under the authority of the Joint Economic Board, which shall be the sole issuing authority and which shall determine the reserves to be held against such currencies.

9. So far as is consistent with paragraph 2 (b) above, each State may operate its own central bank, control its own fiscal and credit policy, its foreign exchange receipts and expenditures, the grant of import licenses, and may conduct international financial operations on its own faith and credit. During the first two years after the termination of the Mandate, the Joint Economic Board shall have the authority to take such measures as may be necessary to ensure that--to the extent that the total foreign exchange revenues of the two States from the export of goods and services permit, and provided that each State takes appropriate measures to conserve its own foreign exchange resources--each State shall have available, in any twelve months' period, foreign exchange sufficient to assure the supply of quantities of imported goods and services for consumption in its territory equivalent to the quantities of such goods and services consumed in that territory in the twelve months' period ending 31 December 1947.

10. All economic authority not specifically vested in the Joint Economic Board is reserved to each State.

11. There shall be a common customs tariff with complete freedom of trade between the States, and between the States and the City of Jerusalem.

12. The tariff schedules shall be drawn up by a Tariff Commission, consisting of representatives of each of the States in equal numbers, and shall be submitted to the Joint Economic Board for approval by a majority vote. In case of disagreement in the Tariff Commission, the Joint Economic Board shall arbitrate the points of difference. In the event that the Tariff Commission fails to draw up any schedule by a date to be fixed, the Joint Economic Board shall determine the tariff schedule.

13. The following items shall be a first charge on the customs and other common revenue of the Joint Economic Board:

(a) The expenses of the customs service and of the operation of the joint services;

(b) The administrative expenses of the Joint Economic Board;

(c) The financial obligations of the Administration of Palestine consisting of:

(i) The service of the outstanding public debt;

(ii) The cost of superannuation benefits, now being paid or falling due in the future, in accordance with the rules and to the extent established by paragraph 3 of chapter 3 above.

14. After these obligations have been met in full, the surplus revenue from the customs and other common services shall be divided in the following manner: not less than 5 per cent and not more than 10 per cent to the City of Jerusalem; the residue shall be allocated to each State by the Joint Economic Board equitably, with the objective of maintaining a sufficient and suitable level of government and social services in each State, except that the share of either State shall not exceed the amount of that State's contribution to the revenues of the Economic Union by more than approximately four million pounds in any year. The amount granted may be adjusted by the Board according to the price level in relation to the prices prevailing at the time of the establishment of the Union. After five years, the principles of the distribution of the joint revenues may be revised by the Joint Economic Board on a basis of equity.

15. All international conventions and treaties affecting customs tariff rates, and those communications services under the jurisdiction of the Joint Economic Board, shall be entered into by both States. In these matters, the two States shall be bound to act in accordance with the majority vote of the Joint Economic Board.

16. The Joint Economic Board shall endeavour to secure for Palestine's export fair and equal access to world markets.

17. All enterprises operated by the Joint Economic Board shall pay fair wages on a uniform basis.

Freedom of transit and visit

18. The undertaking shall contain provisions preserving freedom of transit and visit for all residents or citizens of both States and of the City of Jerusalem, subject to security considerations; provided that each state and the City shall control residence within its borders.

Termination, modification and interpretation of the undertaking

19. The undertaking and any treaty issuing therefrom shall remain in force for a period of ten years. It shall continue in force until notice of termination, to take effect two years thereafter, is given by either of the parties.

20. During the initial ten-year period, the undertaking and any treaty issuing therefrom may not be modified except by consent of both parties and with the approval of the General Assembly.

21. Any dispute relating to the application or the interpretation of the undertaking and any treaty issuing therefrom shall be referred, at the request of either party, to the international Court of Justice, unless the parties agree to another mode of settlement.

E. ASSETS

1. The movable assets of the Administration of Palestine shall be allocated to the Arab and Jewish States and the City of Jerusalem on an equitable basis. Allocations should be made by the United Nations Commission referred to in section B, paragraph 1, above. Immovable assets shall become the property of the government of the territory in which they are situated.

2. During the period between the appointment of the United Nations Commission and the termination of the Mandate, the mandatory Power shall, except in respect of ordinary operations, consult with the Commission on any measure which it may contemplate involving the liquidation, disposal or encumbering of the assets of the Palestine Government, such as the accumulated treasury surplus, the proceeds of Government bond issues, State lands or any other asset.

F. ADMISSION TO MEMBERSHIP IN THE UNITED NATIONS

When the independence of either the Arab or the Jewish State as envisaged in this plan has become effective and the declaration and undertaking, as envisaged in this plan, have been signed by either of them, sympathetic consideration should be given to its application for admission to membership in the United Nations in accordance with Article 4 of the Charter of the United Nations.

PART II. Boundaries

A. THE ARAB STATE

The area of the Arab State in Western Galilee is bounded on the west by the Mediterranean and on the north by the frontier of the Lebanon from Ras en Naqura to a point north of Saliha. From there the boundary proceeds southwards, leaving the built-up area of Saliha in the Arab State, to join the southernmost point of this village. Thence it follows the western boundary line of the villages of `Alma, Rihaniya and Teitaba, thence following the northern boundary line of Meirun village to join the Acre-Safad sub-district boundary line. It follows this line to a point west of Es Sammu'i village and joins it again at the northernmost point of Farradiya. Thence it follows the sub-district boundary line to the Acre-Safad main road. From here it follows the western boundary of Kafr I'nan village until it reaches the Tiberias-Acre sub-district boundary line, passing to the west of the junction of the Acre-Safad and Lubiya-Kafr I'nan roads. From south-west corner of Kafr I'nan village the boundary line follows the western boundary of the Tiberias sub-district to a point close to the boundary line between the villages of Maghar and Eilabun, thence bulging out to the west to include as much of the eastern part of the plain of Battuf as is necessary for the reservoir proposed by the Jewish Agency for the irrigation of lands to the south and east.

The boundary rejoins the Tiberias sub-district boundary at a point on the Nazareth-Tiberias road south-east of the built-up area of Tur'an; thence it runs southwards, at first following the sub-district boundary and then passing between the Kadoorie Agricultural School and Mount Tabor, to a point due south at the base of Mount Tabor. From here it runs due west, parallel to the horizontal grid line 230, to the north-east corner of the village lands of Tel Adashim. It then runs to the north-west corner of these lands, whence it turns south and west so as to include in the Arab State the sources of the Nazareth water supply in Yafa village. On reaching Ginneiger it follows the eastern, northern and western boundaries of the lands of this village to their south-west corner, whence it proceeds in a straight line to a point on the Haifa-Afula railway on the boundary between the villages of Sarid and El Mujeidil. This is the point of intersection.

The south-western boundary of the area of the Arab State in Galilee takes a line from this point, passing northwards along the eastern boundaries of Sarid and Gevat to the north-eastern corner of Nahalal, proceeding thence across the land of Kefar ha Horesh to a central point on the southern boundary of the village of `Ilut, thence westwards along that village boundary to the eastern boundary of Beit Lahm, thence northwards and north-eastwards along its western boundary to the north-eastern corner of Waldheim and thence north-westwards across the village lands of Shafa 'Amr to the south-eastern corner of Ramat Yohanan'. From here it runs due north-north-east to a point on the Shafa 'Amr-Haifa road, west of its junction with the road to I'Billin. From there it proceeds north-east to a point on the southern boundary of I'Billin situated to the west of the I'Billin-Birwa road. Thence along that boundary to its westernmost point, whence it turns to the north, follows across the village land of Tamra to the north-westernmost corner and along the western boundary of Julis until it reaches the Acre-Safad road. It then runs westwards along the southern side of the Safad-Acre road to the Galilee-Haifa District boundary, from which point it follows that boundary to the sea.

The boundary of the hill country of Samaria and Judea starts on the Jordan River at the Wadi Malih south-east of Beisan and runs due west to meet the Beisan-Jericho road and then follows the western side of that road in a north-westerly direction to the junction of the boundaries of the sub-districts of Beisan, Nablus, and Jenin. From that point it follows the Nablus-Jenin sub-district boundary westwards for a distance of about three kilometres and then turns north-westwards, passing to the east of the built-up areas of the villages of Jalbun and Faqqu'a, to the boundary of the sub-districts of Jenin and Beisan at a point north-east of Nuris. Thence it proceeds first north-westwards to a point due north of the built-up area of Zir'in and then westwards to the Afula-Jenin railway, thence north-westwards along the district boundary line to the point of intersection on the Hejaz railway. From here the boundary runs south-westwards, including the built-up area and some of the land of the village of Kh.Lid in the Arab State to cross the Haifa-Jenin road at a point on the district boundary between Haifa and Samaria west of El Mansi. It follows this boundary to the southernmost point of the village of El Buteimat. From here it follows the northern and eastern boundaries of the village of Ar'ara, rejoining the Haifa-Samaria district boundary at Wadi'Ara, and thence proceeding south-south-westwards in an approximately straight line joining up with the western boundary of Qaqun to a point east of the railway line on the eastern boundary of Qaqun village. From here it runs along the railway line some distance to the east of it to a point just east of the Tulkarm railway station. Thence the boundary follows a line half-way between the railway and the Tulkarm-Qalqiliya-Jaljuliya and Ras el Ein road to a point just east of Ras el Ein station, whence it proceeds along the railway some distance to the east of it to the point on the railway line south of the junction of the Haifa-Lydda and Beit Nabala lines, whence it proceeds along the southern border of Lydda airport to its south-west corner, thence in a south-westerly direction to a point just west of the built-up area of Sarafand el'Amar, whence it turns south, passing just to the west of the built-up area of Abu el Fadil to the north-east corner of the lands of Beer Ya'Aqov. (The boundary line should be so demarcated as to allow direct access from the Arab State to the airport.) Thence the boundary line follows the western and southern boundaries of Ramle village, to the north-east corner of El Na'ana village, thence in a straight line to the southernmost point of El Barriya, along the eastern boundary of that village and the southern boundary of 'Innaba village. Thence it turns north to follow the southern side of the Jaffa-Jerusalem road until El Qubab, whence it follows the road to the boundary of Abu Shusha. It runs along the eastern boundaries of Abu Shusha, Seidun, Hulda to the southernmost point of Hulda, thence westwards in a straight line to the north-eastern corner of Umm Kalkha, thence following the northern boundaries of Umm Kalkha, Qazaza and the northern and western boundaries of Mukhezin to the Gaza District boundary and thence runs across the village lands of El Mismiya, El Kabira, and Yasur to the southern point of intersection, which is midway between the built-up areas of Yasur and Batani Sharqi.

From the southern point of intersection the boundary lines run north-westwards between the villages of Gan Yavne and Barqa to the sea at a point half way between Nabi Yunis and Minat el Qila, and south-eastwards to a point west of Qastina, whence it turns in a south-westerly direction, passing to the east of the built-up areas of Es Sawafir, Es Sharqiya and Ibdis. From the south-east corner of Ibdis village it runs to a point south-west of the built-up area of Beit 'Affa, crossing the Hebron-El Majdal road just to the west of the built-up area of Iraq Suweidan. Thence it proceeds southwards along the western village boundary of El

Faluja to the Beersheba sub-district boundary. It then runs across the tribal lands of 'Arab el Jubarat to a point on the boundary between the sub-districts of Beersheba and Hebron north of Kh. Khuweilifa, whence it proceeds in a south-westerly direction to a point on the Beersheba-Gaza main road two kilometres to the north-west of the town. It then turns south-eastwards to reach Wadi Sab' at a point situated one kilometre to the west of it. From here it turns north-eastwards and proceeds along Wadi Sab' and along the Beersheba-Hebron road for a distance of one kilometre, whence it turns eastwards and runs in a straight line to Kh. Kuseifa to join the Beersheba-Hebron sub-district boundary. It then follows the Beersheba-Hebron boundary eastwards to a point north of Ras Ez Zuweira, only departing from it so as to cut across the base of the indentation between vertical grid lines 150 and 160.

About five kilometres north-east of Ras ez Zuweira it turns north, excluding from the Arab State a strip along the coast of the Dead Sea not more than seven kilometres in depth, as far as Ein Geddi, whence it turns due east to join the Transjordan frontier in the Dead Sea.

The northern boundary of the Arab section of the coastal plain runs from a point between Minat el Qila and Nabi Yunis, passing between the built-up areas of Gan Yavne and Barqa to the point of intersection. From here it turns south-westwards, running across the lands of Batani Sharqi, along the eastern boundary of the lands of Beit Daras and across the lands of Julis, leaving the built-up areas of Batani Sharqi and Julis to the westwards, as far as the north-west corner of the lands of Beit Tima. Thence it runs east of El Jiya across the village lands of El Barbara along the eastern boundaries of the villages of Beit Jirja, Deir Suneid and Dimra. From the south-east corner of Dimra the boundary passes across the lands of Beit Hanun, leaving the Jewish lands of Nir-Am to the eastwards. From the south-east corner of Dimra the boundary passes across the lands of Beit Hanun, leaving the Jewish lands of Nir-Am to the eastwards. From the south-east corner of Beit Hanun the line runs south-west to a point south of the parallel grid line 100, then turns north-west for two kilometres, turning again in a south-westerly direction and continuing in an almost straight line to the north-west corner of the village lands of Kirbet Ikhza'a. From there it follows the boundary line of this village to its southernmost point. It then runs in a southernly direction along the vertical grid line 90 to its junction with the horizontal grid line 70. It then turns south-eastwards to Kh. el Ruheiba and then proceeds in a southerly direction to a point known as El Baha, beyond which it crosses the Beersheba-El 'Auja main road to the west of Kh. el Mushrifa. From there it joins Wadi El Zaiyatin just to the west of El Subeita. From there it turns to the north-east and then to the south-east following this Wadi and passes to the east of 'Abda to join Wadi Nafkh. It then bulges to the south-west along Wadi Nafkh. It then bulges to the south-west along Wadi Nafkh, Wadi Ajrim and Wadi Lassan to the point where Wadi Lassan crosses the Egyptian frontier.

The area of the Arab enclave of Jaffa consists of that part of the town-planning area of Jaffa which lies to the west of the Jewish quarters lying south of Tel-Aviv, to the west of the continuation of Herzl street up to its junction with the Jaffa-Jerusalem road, to the south-west of the section of the Jaffa-Jerusalem road lying south-east of that junction, to the west of Miqve Israel lands, to the north-west of Holon local council area, to the north of the line linking up the north-west corner of Holon with the north-east corner of Bat Yam local council area and to the north of Bat Yam local council area. The question of Karton quarter will be decided by the Boundary Commission, bearing in mind among other considerations the desirability of including the smallest possible number of its Arab inhabitants and the largest possible number of its Jewish inhabitants in the Jewish State.

B. THE JEWISH STATE

The north-eastern sector of the Jewish State (Eastern) Galilee) is bounded on the north and west by the Lebanese frontier and on the east by the frontiers of Syria and Transjordan. It includes the whole of the Hula Basin, Lake Tiberias, the whole of the Beisan sub-district, the boundary line being extended to the crest of the Gilboa mountains and the Wadi Malih. From there the Jewish State extends north-west, following the boundary described in respect of the Arab State.

The Jewish Section of the coastal plain extends from a point between Minat et Qila and Nabi Yunis in the Gaza sub-district and includes the towns of Haifa and Tel-Aviv, leaving Jaffa as an enclave of the Arab State. The eastern frontier of the Jewish State follows the boundary described in respect of the Arab State.

The Beersheba area comprises the whole of the Beersheba sub-district, including the Negeb and the eastern part of the Gaza sub-district, but excluding the town of Beersheba and those areas described in respect of the Arab State. It includes also a strip of land along the Dead Sea stretching from the Beersheba-Hebron sub-district boundary line to Ein Geddi, as described in respect of the Arab State.

C. THE CITY OF JERUSALEM

The boundaries of the City of Jerusalem are as defined in the recommendations on the City of Jerusalem. (See Part III, Section B, below).

PART III. City of Jerusalem

A. SPECIAL REGIME

The City of Jerusalem shall be established as a corpus separatum under a special international regime and shall be administered by the United Nations. The Trusteeship Council shall be designated to discharge the responsibilities of the Administering Authority on behalf of the United Nations.

B. BOUNDARIES OF THE CITY

The City of Jerusalem shall include the present municipality of Jerusalem plus the surrounding villages and towns, the most eastern of which shall be Abu Dis; the most southern, Bethlehem; the most western, Ein Karim (including also the built-up area of Motsa); and the most northern Shu'fat, as indicated on the attached sketch-map (annex B).

C. STATUTE OF THE CITY

The Trusteeship Council shall, within five months of the approval of the present plan, elaborate and approve a detailed Statute of the City which shall contain inter alia the substance of the following provisions:

1. Government machinery; special objectives. The Administering Authority in discharging its administrative obligations shall pursue the following special objectives:

(a) To protect and to preserve the unique spiritual and religious interests located in the city of the three great monotheistic faiths throughout the world, Christian, Jewish and Moslem; to this end to ensure that order and peace, and especially religious peace, reign in Jerusalem;

(b) To foster co-operation among all the inhabitants of the city in their own interests as well as in order to encourage and support the peaceful development of the mutual relations between the two Palestinian peoples throughout the Holy Land; to promote the security, well-being and any constructive measures of development of the residents, having regard to the special circumstances and customs of the various peoples and communities.

2. Governor and administrative staff. A Governor of the City of Jerusalem shall be appointed by the Trusteeship Council and shall be responsible to it. He shall be selected on the basis of special qualifications and without regard to nationality. He shall not, however, be a citizen of either State in Palestine.

The Governor shall represent the United Nations in the City and shall exercise on their behalf all powers of administration, including the conduct of external affairs. He shall be assisted by an administrative staff classed as international officers in the meaning of Article 100 of the Charter and chosen whenever practicable from the residents of the city and of the rest of Palestine on a non-discriminatory basis. A detailed plan for the organization of the administration of the city shall be submitted by the Governor to the Trusteeship Council and duly approved by it.

3. Local autonomy. (a) The existing local autonomous units in the territory of the city (villages, townships and municipalities) shall enjoy wide powers of local government and administration.

(b) The Governor shall study and submit for the consideration and decision of the Trusteeship Council a plan for the establishment of a special town units consisting respectively, of the Jewish and Arab sections of new Jerusalem. The new town units shall continue to form part of the present municipality of Jerusalem.

4. Security measures. (a) The City of Jerusalem shall be demilitarized; its neutrality shall be declared and preserved, and no para-military formations, exercises or activities shall be permitted within its borders.

(b) Should the administration of the City of Jerusalem be seriously obstructed or prevented by the non-co-operation or interference of one or more sections of the population, the Governor shall have authority to take such measures as may be necessary to restore the effective functioning of the administration.

(c) To assist in the maintenance of internal law and order and especially for the protection of the Holy Places and religious buildings and sites in the city, the Governor shall organize a special police force of adequate strength, the members of which shall be recruited outside of Palestine. The Governor shall be empowered to direct such budgetary provision as may be necessary for the maintenance of this force.

5. Legislative organization. A Legislative Council, elected by adult residents of the city irrespective of nationality on the basis of universal and secret suffrage and proportional representation, shall have powers of legislation and taxation. No legislative measures shall, however, conflict or interfere with the provisions which will be set forth in the Statute of the City, nor shall any law, regulation, or official action prevail over them. The Statute shall grant to the Governor a right of vetoing bills inconsistent with the provisions referred to in the preceding sentence. It shall also empower him to promulgate temporary ordinances in case the council fails to adopt in time a bill deemed essential to the normal functioning of the administration.

6. Administration of justice. The Statute shall provide for the establishment of an independent judiciary system, including a court of appeal. All the inhabitants of the City shall be subject to it.

7. Economic union and economic regime. The City of Jerusalem shall be included in the Economic Union of Palestine and be bound by all stipulations of the undertaking and of any treaties issued therefrom, as well as by the decision of the Joint Economic Board. The headquarters of the Economic Board shall be established in the territory of the City.

The Statute shall provide for the regulation of economic matters not falling within the regime of the Economic Union, on the basis of equal treatment and non-discrimination for all members of the United Nations and their nationals.

8. Freedom of transit and visit; control of residents. Subject to considerations of security, and of economic welfare as determined by the Governor under the directions of the Trusteeship Council, freedom of entry into, and residence within, the borders of the City shall be guaranteed for the residents or citizens of the Arab and Jewish States. Immigration into, and residence within, the borders of the city for nationals of other States shall be controlled by the Governor under the directions of the Trusteeship Council.

9. Relations with the Arab and Jewish States. Representatives of the Arab and Jewish States shall be accredited to the Governor of the City and charged with the protection of the interests of their States and nationals in connexion with the international administration of the City.

10. Official languages. Arabic and Hebrew shall be the official languages of the city. This will not preclude the adoption of one or more additional working languages, as may be required.

11. Citizenship. All the residents shall become ipso facto citizens of the City of Jerusalem unless they opt for citizenship of the State of which they have been citizens or, if Arabs or Jews, have filed notice of intention to become citizens of the Arab or Jewish State respectively, according to part I, section B, paragraph 9, of this plan.

The Trusteeship Council shall make arrangements for consular protection of the citizens of the City outside its territory.

12. Freedoms of Citizens. (a) Subject only to the requirements of public order and morals, the inhabitants of the City shall be ensured the enjoyment of human rights and fundamental freedoms, including freedom of conscience, religion and worship, language, education, speech and press, assembly and association, and petition.

(b) No discrimination of any kind shall be made between the inhabitants on the grounds of race, religion, language or sex.

(c) All persons within the City shall be entitled to equal protection of the laws.

(d) The family law and personal status of the various persons and communities and their religious interests, including endowments, shall be respected.

(e) Except as may be required for the maintenance of public order and good government, no measure shall be taken to obstruct or interfere with the enterprise of religious or charitable bodies of all faiths or to discriminate against any representative or member of these bodies on the ground of his religion or nationality.

(f) The City shall ensure adequate primary and secondary education for the Arab and Jewish communities respectively, in their own languages and in accordance with their cultural traditions.

The right of each community to maintain its own schools for the education of its own members in its own language, while conforming to such educational requirements of a general nature as the City may impose, shall not be denied or impaired. Foreign educational establishments shall continue their activity on the basis of their existing rights.

(g) No restriction shall be imposed on the free use by any inhabitant of the City of any language in private intercourse, in commerce, in religion, in the Press or in publications of any kind, or at public meetings.

13. Holy Places. (a) Existing rights in respect of Holy Places and religious buildings or sites shall not be denied or impaired.

(b) Free access to the Holy Places and religious buildings or sites and the free exercise of worship shall be secured in conformity with existing rights and subject to the requirements of public order and decorum.

(c) Holy Places and religious buildings or sites shall be preserved. No act shall be permitted which may in any way impair their sacred character. If at any time it appears to the Governor that any particular Holy Place, religious building or site is in need of urgent repair, the Governor may call upon the community or communities concerned to carry out such repair. The Governor may carry it out himself at the expense of the community or communities concerned if no action is taken within a reasonable time.

(d) No taxation shall be levied in respect of any Holy Place, religious building or site which was exempt from taxation on the date of the creation of the City. No change in the incidence of such taxation shall be made which would either discriminate between the owners or occupiers of Holy Places, religious buildings or sites, or would place such owners or occupiers in a position less favourable in relation to the general incidence of taxation than existed at the time of the adoption of the Assembly's recommendations.

14. Special powers of the Governor in respect of the Holy Places, religious buildings and sites in the City and in any part of Palestine. (a) The protection of the Holy Places, religious buildings and sites located in the City of Jerusalem shall be a special concern of the Governor.

(b) With relation to such places, buildings and sites in Palestine outside the city, the Governor shall determine, on the ground of powers granted to him by the Constitutions of both States, whether the provisions of the Constitutions of the Arab and Jewish States in Palestine dealing therewith and the religious rights appertaining thereto are being properly applied and respected.

(c) The Governor shall also be empowered to make decisions on the basis of existing rights in cases of disputes which may arise between the different religious communities or the rites of a religious community in respect of the Holy Places, religious buildings and sites in any part of Palestine.

In this task he may be assisted by a consultative council of representatives of different denominations acting in an advisory capacity.

D. DURATION OF THE SPECIAL REGIME

The Statute elaborated by the Trusteeship Council on the aforementioned principles shall come into force not later than 1 October 1948. It shall remain in force in the first instance for a period of ten years, unless the Trusteeship Council finds it necessary to undertake a re-examination of these provisions at an earlier date. After the expiration of this period the whole scheme shall be subject to re-examination by the Trusteeship Council in the light of the experience acquired with its functioning. The residents of the City shall be then free to express by means of a referendum their wishes as to possible modifications of the regime of the City.

PART IV. CAPITULATIONS

States whose nationals have in the past enjoyed in Palestine the privileges and immunities of foreigners, including the benefits of consular jurisdiction and protection, as formerly enjoyed by capitulation or usage in the Ottoman Empire, are invited to renounce any right pertaining to them to the re-establishment of such privileges and immunities in the proposed Arab and Jewish States and the City of Jerusalem.

UN General Assembly Resolution 194 (III)

A/RES/194 (III)
11 December 1948

194 (III). Palestine -- Progress Report of the United Nations Mediator

The General Assembly,
Having considered further the situation in Palestine,

1. Expresses its deep appreciation of the progress achieved through the good offices of the late United Nations Mediator in promoting a peaceful adjustment of the future situation of Palestine, for which cause he sacrificed his life; and

Extends its thanks to the Acting Mediator and his staff for their continued efforts and devotion to duty in Palestine;

2. Establishes a Conciliation Commission consisting of three States members of the United Nations which shall have the following functions:

(a) To assume, in so far as it considers necessary in existing circumstances, the functions given to the United Nations Mediator on Palestine by resolution 186 (S-2) of the General Assembly of 14 May 1948;

(b) To carry out the specific functions and directives given to it by the present resolution and such additional functions and directives as may be given to it by the General Assembly or by the Security Council;

(c) To undertake, upon the request of the Security Council, any of the functions now assigned to the United Nations Mediator on Palestine or to the United Nations Truce Commission by resolutions of the Security Council; upon such request to the Conciliation Commission by the Security Council with respect to all the remaining functions of the United Nations Mediator on Palestine under Security Council resolutions, the office of the Mediator shall be terminated;

3. Decides that a Committee of the Assembly, consisting of China, France, the Union of Soviet Socialist Republics, the United Kingdom and the United States of America, shall present, before the end of the first

part of the present session of the General Assembly, for the approval of the Assembly, a proposal concerning the names of the three States which will constitute the Conciliation Commission;

4. Requests the Commission to begin its functions at once, with a view to the establishment of contact between the parties themselves and the Commission at the earliest possible date;

5. Calls upon the Governments and authorities concerned to extend the scope of the negotiations provided for in the Security Council's resolution of 16 November 1948 and to seek agreement by negotiations conducted either with the Conciliation Commission or directly, with a view to the final settlement of all questions outstanding between them;

6. Instructs the Conciliation Commission to take steps to assist the Governments and authorities concerned to achieve a final settlement of all questions outstanding between them;

7. Resolves that the Holy Places - including Nazareth - religious buildings and sites in Palestine should be protected and free access to them assured, in accordance with existing rights and historical practice; that arrangements to this end should be under effective United Nations supervision; that the United Nations Conciliation Commission, in presenting to the fourth regular session of the General Assembly its detailed proposals for a permanent international regime for the territory of Jerusalem, should include recommendations concerning the Holy Places in that territory; that with regard to the Holy Places in the rest of Palestine the Commission should call upon the political authorities of the areas concerned to give appropriate formal guarantees as to the protection of the Holy Places and access to them; and that these undertakings should be presented to the General Assembly for approval;

8. Resolves that, in view of its association with three world religions, the Jerusalem area, including the present municipality of Jerusalem plus the surrounding villages and towns, the most eastern of which shall be Abu Dis; the most southern, Bethlehem; the most western, Ein Karim (including also the built-up area of Motsa); and the most northern, Shu'fat, should be accorded special and separate treatment from the rest of Palestine and should be placed under effective United Nations control;

Requests the Security Council to take further steps to ensure the demilitarization of Jerusalem at the earliest possible date;

Instructs the Conciliation Commission to present to the fourth regular session of the General Assembly detailed proposals for a permanent international regime for the Jerusalem area which will provide for the maximum local autonomy for distinctive groups consistent with the special international status of the Jerusalem area;

The Conciliation Commission is authorized to appoint a United Nations representative, who shall co-operate with the local authorities with respect to the interim administration of the Jerusalem area;

9. Resolves that, pending agreement on more detailed arrangements among the Governments and authorities concerned, the freest possible access to Jerusalem by road, rail or air should be accorded to all inhabitants of Palestine;

Instructs the Conciliation Commission to report immediately to the Security Council, for appropriate action by that organ, any attempt by any party to impede such access;

10. Instructs the Conciliation Commission to seek arrangements among the Governments and authorities concerned which will facilitate the economic development of the area, including arrangements for access to ports and airfields and the use of transportation and communication facilities;

11. Resolves that the refugees wishing to return to their homes and live at peace with their neighbours should be permitted to do so at the earliest practicable date, and that compensation should be paid for the property of those choosing not to return and for loss of or damage to property which, under principles of international law or in equity, should be made good by the Governments or authorities responsible;

Instructs the Conciliation Commission to facilitate the repatriation, resettlement and economic and social rehabilitation of the refugees and the payment of compensation, and to maintain close relations with the Director of the United Nations Relief for Palestine Refugees and, through him, with the appropriate organs and agencies of the United Nations;

12. Authorizes the Conciliation Commission to appoint such subsidiary bodies and to employ such technical experts, acting under its authority, as it may find necessary for the effective discharge of its functions and responsibilities under the present resolution;

The Conciliation Commission will have its official headquarters at Jerusalem. The authorities responsible for maintaining order in Jerusalem will be responsible for taking all measures necessary to ensure the security of the Commission. The Secretary-General will provide a limited number of guards to the protection of the staff and premises of the Commission;

13. Instructs the Conciliation Commission to render progress reports periodically to the Secretary-General for transmission to the Security Council and to the Members of the United Nations;

14. Calls upon all Governments and authorities concerned to co-operate with the Conciliation Commission and to take all possible steps to assist in the implementation of the present resolution;

15. Requests the Secretary-General to provide the necessary staff and facilities and to make appropriate arrangements to provide the necessary funds required in carrying out the terms of the present resolution.

* * *

At the 186th plenary meeting on 11 December 1948, a committee of the Assembly consisting of the five States designated in paragraph 3 of the above resolution proposed that the following three States should constitute the Conciliation Commission:

France, Turkey, United States of America.

The proposal of the Committee having been adopted by the General Assembly at the same meeting, the Conciliation Commission is therefore composed of the above-mentioned three States.

Bibliography

Brynen, Rex, and Bassel F. Salloukh, eds. 2004. *Persistent Permeability? Regionalism, Localism, and Globalization in the Middle East.* Burlington, VT: Ashgate Publishing Limited.

Clark, Tom. 2004. *The Global Refugee Regime: Charity, Management and Human Rights.* Victoria, BC: Trafford Publishing.

Feller, Erika, Volker Turk, and Frances Nicholson, eds. 2003. *Refugee Protection in International Law: UNHCR's Global Consultations on International Protection.* New York, NY: Cambridge University Press.

Hourani, Albert. 1991. *A History of the Arab Peoples.* Cambridge, MA: The Belknap Press of Harvard University Press.

Lischer, Sarah Kenyon. 2005. *Dangerous Sanctuaries: Refugee Camps, Civil War, and the Dilemmas of Humanitarian Aid.* Ithica, NY: Cornell University Press.

Musalo, Karen, Moore, Jennifer, and Boswell, Richard A. 2002. *Refugee Law and Policy: A Comparative and International Approach, 2nd Edition.* Durham, NC: Carolina Academic Press.

Morris, Benny. 2004. *The Birth of the Palestinian Refugee Problem Revisited.* Cambridge, UK: Cambridge University Press, Cambridge Middle East Studies.

United Nations. 1948. *Universal Declaration of Human Rights.* General Assembly Resolution 217 A (III). United Nations High Commissioner for Refugees. 2006. Division of External Relations.

The State of the World's Refugee's 2006. New York, NY: Oxford University Press.

United Nations High Commissioner for Refugees. 2006. *Convention and Protocol Relating to the Status of Refugees.* http://www.unhcr.org/protect/PROTECTION/3b66c2aa10.pdf

United Nations High Commissioner for Refugees. 2007. UNHCR Briefing
    Notes. *Gulf of Aden: More drowned by smugglers, others die of
    asphyxia and dehydration.* April 24, 2007.
    http://www.unhcr.org/news/NEWS/462ddf222.html

United Nations High Commissioner for Refugees. 2006. *Jordan 2006
    Country Operations Plan.*
    http://www.unhcr.org/home/RSDCOI/43327b4e2.pdf

United Nations High Commissioner for Refugees. 2002. *Safe Avenues to
    Asylum? The Actual and Potential Role of EU Diplomatic
    Representations in Processing Asylum Requests.*
    http://www.unhcr.org/partners/PARTNERS/3cd000a52.pdf

United Nations High Commissioner for Refugees. 2006. *UNCHR and
    International Protection: A Protection Induction Programme.*
    http://www.unhcr.org/static/publ/ba2007/ga2007toc.htm

United Nations High Commissioner for Refugees. 2006. *UNHCR Global
    Appeal 2007.*
    http://www.unhcr.org/static/publ/ga2007/ga2007toc.htm

United Nations High Commissioner for Refugees. 2007. *Yemen 2007
    Country Operations Plan.*
    http://www.unhcr.org/home/RSDCOI/4522204c2.pdf

United States Central Intelligence Agency. 2007. *CIA World Factbook.*
    https://www.cia.gov/cia/publications/factbook/

Zaiotti, Ruben. 2006. Dealing with non-Palestinian Refugees in the
    Middle East; Policies and Practices in an Uncertain Environment.
    International Journal of Refugee Law. 18: 333-353.